1985

Self-Directed Learning: From Theory to Practice

Stephen Brookfield, *Editor*

NEW DIRECTIONS FOR CONTINUING EDUCATION

GORDON G. DARKENWALD, *Editor-in-Chief*
ALAN B. KNOX, *Consulting Editor*

Number 25, March 1985

Paperback sourcebooks in
The Jossey-Bass Higher Education Series

Jossey-Bass Inc., Publishers
San Francisco • Washington • London

Stephen Brookfield (Ed.).
Self-Directed Learning: From Theory to Practice.
New Directions for Continuing Education, no. 25.
San Francisco: Jossey-Bass, 1985.

New Directions for Continuing Education Series
Gordon G. Darkenwald, *Editor-in-Chief*
Alan B. Knox, *Consulting Editor*

New Directions for Continuing Education (publication number
USPS 493-930) quarterly by Jossey-Bass Inc., Publishers.
Second-class postage rates paid at San Francisco, California,
and at additional mailing offices.

Correspondence:
Subscriptions, single-issue orders, change of address notices, undelivered
copies, and other correspondence should be sent to Subscriptions,
Jossey-Bass Inc., Publishers, 433 California Street, San Francisco
California 94104.

Editorial correspondence should be sent to the managing
Editor-in-Chief, Gordon G. Darkenwald, Graduate School
of Education, Rutgers University, 10 Seminary Place,
New Brunswick, New Jersey 08903.

Library of Congress Catalogue Card Number LC 84-82368

International Standard Serial Number ISSN 0195-2242

International Standard Book Number ISBN 87589-743-6

Cover art by Willi Baum

Manufactured in the United States of America

Ordering Information

The paperback sourcebooks listed below are published quarterly and can be ordered either by subscription or single-copy.

Subscriptions cost $35.00 per year for institutions, agencies, and libraries. Individuals can subscribe at the special rate of $25.00 per year *if payment is by personal check.* (Note that the full rate of $35.00 applies if payment is by institutional check, even if the subscription is designated for an individual.) Standing orders are accepted. Subscriptions normally begin with the first of the four sourcebooks in the current publication year of the series. When ordering, please indicate if you prefer your subscription to begin with the first issue of the *coming* year.

Single copies are available at $8.95 when payment accompanies order, and *all single-copy orders under $25.00 must include payment.* (California, New Jersey, New York, and Washington, D.C., residents please include appropriate sales tax.) For billed orders, cost per copy is $8.95 plus postage and handling. (Prices subject to change without notice.)

Bulk orders (ten or more copies) of any individual sourcebook are available at the following discounted prices: 10–49 copies, $8.05 each; 50–100 copies, $7.15 each; over 100 copies, *inquire.* Sales tax and postage and handling charges apply as for single copy orders.

To ensure correct and prompt delivery, all orders must give either the *name of an individual* or an *official purchase order number.* Please submit your order as follows:

Subscriptions: specify series and year subscription is to begin.
Single Copies: specify sourcebook code (such as, CE8) and first two words of title.

Mail orders for United States and Possessions, Latin America, Canada, Japan, Australia, and New Zealand to:
Jossey-Bass Inc., Publishers
433 California Street
San Francisco, California 94104

Mail orders for all other parts of the world to:
Jossey-Bass Limited
28 Banner Street
London EC1Y 8QE

New Directions for Continuing Education Series
Gordon G. Darkenwald, *Editor-in-Chief*
Alan B. Knox, Consulting Editor

Contents

Editor's Notes

Self-directed learning is an idea that, at least in the world of continuing education, has come of age. Although the idea can hardly be described as new, it is only recently that the writings of a body of researchers, scholars, and practitioners have thrown this concept into sharp relief. One idea that underlies much current continuing education philosophy and practice and that is present in the writings of such theorists as Eduard Lindeman and Lyman Bryson early in this century has occupied the attention of significant numbers of continuing educators over the last two decades.

The 1960s and the early 1970s were a time of research. Continuing educators in Canada, America, and Britain began to hear of investigations which claimed that adults typically spent five or seven hundred hours in self-directed learning each year. It was also claimed that much of this learning was effective and enjoyable, not the trouble-strewn path of haphazard and serendipitous circumstance that some professional educators would have liked to believe. This research gave considerable comfort to the deschoolers, who argued that communities contained sufficient knowledge banks, skill models, consultants, and natural learning webs to make abolition of formal schooling seem a real possibility.

At around the same time, a number of related practical initiatives began to occur. The concept of open learning became fashionable, and with the establishment of the British Open University came a number of smaller-scale analogues. The Open Learning Institute in British Columbia was one with which this writer is familiar. Another related innovation was the recognition by some institutions of higher education that knowledge and skills gained by adults through work and community activities might qualify for credit remission in formal courses. Thomas Edison College in Trenton, New Jersey, was a leader is assisting adults to develop portfolios that documented prior experiential learning.

During the 1960s and early 1970s, then, it became evident that many of our stereotypical expectations about the nature and extent of adult learning and about the appropriate role for the professional educator were being challenged or contradicted. The ability and readiness of many adults to conduct self-directed learning projects became generally accepted. Concurrent with this development, a number of energetic practitioners began to explore ways of building bridges between the world of formal adult education and the activities of self-directed learners.

As we near the middle of the present decade, researchers and practitioners have had some time to reflect on the last twenty years of work in the field of self-directed learning. At times, we have come close to accepting an

1

academic orthodoxy just as dangerous as the earlier notion that students were the passive recipients of knowledge transmitted by bountiful experts. This new orthodoxy asserted that all adults were natural, self-directed learners and that the task of the adult educator was simply to release the boundless, peerless capacity for self-directed learning that was innate but dormant in all adults.

Those of us who have tried to liberate the genie of self-directed learning from the bodies and minds of adults in our professional sphere of influence have soon realized that the new orthodoxy is dangerously oversimplified. Far from acquiescing in the joyful release of latent talents for self-directedness, many adults stubbornly resisted our efforts. Others were visibly intimidated by injunctions to take control of their own learning. Still others were confused or puzzled by educators who urged students to be self-directed while retaining control over the criteria by which students' success was to be judged.

One purpose of this volume is to take stock of our experience of trying to transfer principles of self-directed learning to our educational practice. It is common enough to hear educators declare that they promote self-directed learning in their students. However, it is uncommon to find any detailed evidence of how they did so or of how institutional constraints or students' unreadiness for taking control over learning created problems for them. It is not easy to admit that a dearly held, humanistically impeccable philosophy might be difficult to implement in practical situations.

In the chapters of this volume, experienced practitioners, researchers, and theorists document their attempts to introduce principles of self-directed learning into their work with adult learners. We have a plethora of research reports attesting to the extent of self-directed learning within the adult population. We also have any number of philosophical declarations holding the purpose of adult education to be the enhancement of adults' powers of self-directedness. Thus, what we need are some critical and honest accounts of attempts to work with adults in a self-directed mode from within institutional settings. No adult can be fully self-directed while working within an accredited educational institution. It is possible, however, to be creative in introducing elements of self-directedness into needs assessment, curriculum development, educational process, and evaluation. The accounts gathered in this volume explore the pains and pleasures incurred in such creative innovation.

Chapter One reviews the research and theory in this field and highlights the culture- and class-specific generalizability of much of this research. In Chapter Two, Jack Mezirow continues this critical theme by arguing that self-directedness is essential in adults' attempts to become critically aware of the assumptions underlying their values and behaviors and that it is realized in their attempts to change their lives. Chapter Three concludes this opening section of the book by introducing the topic of how practitioners and theorists can bridge the gap between theory and practice. Ralph Brockett and Roger Hiemstra address facilitator roles, policy implications, and ethical issues.

The next three chapters are case studies of self-directed learning in practice. In Chapter Four, Barbara Bauer describes the AEGIS program at Teachers College, in which self-directed learning principles are the foundation of doctoral study. In Chapter Five, David Carr explores the possibilities for self-directed learning that cultural institutions offer. Museums, libraries, and other institutions are doing much to enhance their educational potential. In Chapter Six, Carol Reed Ash examines one major growth area for the application of self-directed learning, the health professions. She describes a number of initiatives, then focuses on an orientation program for nurses that is organized according to self-directed principles.

Chapter Seven reviews the ethical and professional imperatives affecting the work of continuing educators with self-directed learners in community settings. An account of one project to assist self-directed learners from within a professional, institutional context is given. Chapter Eight concludes the volume with a review of sources that should interest readers who wish to explore this area further.

Stephen Brookfield
Editor

*Stephen Brookfield is assistant professor of adult and continuing
education and associate director of the Center for Adult Education
at Teachers College, Columbia University, New York City. He has
researched the activities of self-directed learners at the University of
Leicester (England), the University of British Columbia (Canada),
and Columbia University (New York). He uses self-directed learning
principles in his work at Teachers College, and he is the author
of* Adult Learners, Adult Education, and the Community
(Teachers College Press, 1983).

Self-directed learning comprises a major area of research and theory in adult education, yet the studies conducted have a culture- and class-specific level of generalizability.

Self-Directed Learning: A Critical Review of Research

Stephen Brookfield

Much like any other field of study, continuing education passes through identifiable periods during which distinctive paradigms of thought and practice are discernible. The decade of the 1970s was undoubtedly the period of self-directed learning characterized as it was by a plethora of empirical studies and by the efforts of Malcolm Knowles (1975) and Allen Tough (1979) to popularize the concept. Any number of indicators can be cited to illustrate the contemporary popularity of the term. The Commission of Professors of Adult Education voted in 1982 to establish a task force on self-directed learning. The pioneering efforts of Allen Tough, represented by his study of the self-teaching activities of Toronto graduates (Tough, 1967), have been replicated in some form in more than fifty follow-up studies. The Self-Directed Learning Readiness Scale (SDLRS) developed by Guglielmino (1977) is often used to measure adults' preparedness for self-directed learning.

As a result, we are in danger of accepting uncritically a new academic orthodoxy in adult education. Put simply, it is not uncommon to hear practitioners and theorists declaring as self-evident a number of doubtful propositions that make self-directed learning the goal and method of adult education. We repeatedly encounter the claim that adults are self-directed. This claim is often speedily followed by the self-contradictory proposition that continuing education should therefore be concerned with developing adults' powers of

S. Brookfield (Ed.). *Self-Directed Learning: From Theory to Practice.* New Directions for Continuing Education, no. 25. San Francisco: Jossey-Bass, March 1985.

self-direction. Self-directed learners are said to be so in control of their learning that those who teach adults are merely resource persons whose role is to facilitate this learning.

If followed to its logical conclusion, this position condemns adults to conduct self-directed learning projects within their own, often narrowly defined, frameworks of thought and action. If the educator is restricted from presenting the adult with alternative ways of interpreting the world or of creating new personal and collective futures, then the educator becomes a kind of master technician who operates within a moral vacuum. While the educator is allowed a role in assisting students to refine their techniques of self-directed learning, that educator is constrained from offering value systems, ideologies, behavioral codes, or images of the future that the adult has yet to encounter.

The reasons for the uncritical and ready acceptance of this academic orthodoxy are probably rooted in the professional insecurity of continuing educators. Embracing this concept without critically scrutinizing its utility means that a potentially useful concept, which possesses some explanatory power and which can become the focus of a purposeful research effort, is in danger of being debased by frequent and arbitrary use. The enthusiasm of continuing educators for the concept no doubt reflects their longing for a bona fide professional identity. If we can identify a set of learning behaviors that are unmistakably adult, then we have created for ourselves a professional raison d'être. If adults and children exhibit certain empirically verifiable differences in learning style, then we can lay claim to a substantive area for research and practice that is unchallengeably the domain of continuing education. The confident staking of such a claim would be cause for professional celebration. It would provide continuing educators with a professional identity, and it would sustain us against the insecurity and defensiveness that frequently assail us when we are accused of practicing a nondiscipline.

In this chapter, I propose to subject research and theory in this area to close and critical scrutiny. I consider the conceptual soundness of the term and elaborate a definition of self-directed learning that may enable us to identify a mode of learning that is unmistakably adult. The exploration begun here is extended by Jack Mezirow in the next chapter. In this chapter, I also raise some questions about the methodological rigor of the studies on which the new academic orthodoxy is based. The limited nature of the sampling frame for this research and the data collection procedures most frequently used pose limitations that too often are overlooked.

It is important to record the considerable contributions made by researchers in this field to the discipline of continuing education. The efforts of Tough, Knowles, and others have forced professional continuing educators to consider the activities and circumstances of individual adult learners. We can no longer equate the entire practice and performance of adult education with program planning, classroom management, and marketing skills. Instead, we must consider the process by which adults learn in a range of settings, and we must address what we can do to help those individuals to conduct successful learning efforts.

Self-directed learning theorists and researchers have prompted us to challenge the assumption that adult learning can occur only in the presence of an accredited and professionally certified teacher. They have also been instrumental in helping to dispel the false dichotomy between institutionally arranged learning, which is seen as rational, purposeful, and effective, and learning in informal settings, which is viewed as serendipitous, ineffective, and of a lower order. As continuing educators, we have been forced to heed the informal and noninstitutional dimensions of our field.

Self-Directed Learning and Social Settings

The concept of self-directed learning has connotations of autonomy, independence, and isolation, and it is easy to conceive of the self-directed learner as one who pursues learning with a minimum of assistance from external sources. Indeed, individual control over learning is often claimed to be the distinctive characteristic of self-directed learning.

On reflection, however, it is evident that no act of learning can be self-directed if we understand self-direction as meaning the absence of external sources of assistance. Tough (1967, 1979) has repeatedly highlighted the strong reliance on external resources, both human and material, in the conduct of learning projects and pointed out that adults generally say that they would like more, rather than less, assistance in their learning pursuits. Farquharson (1975) and Brookfield (1980, 1981) have documented the manner in which community groups, hobbyists' societies, and other learning networks form the context within which many self-directed learning projects are undertaken.

Moore (1973, p. 669) has argued that the self-directed learner should not be thought of as "an intellectual Robinson Crusoe, castaway and shut off in self-sufficiency." In the pursuit of skills, knowledge, and insight, adults come into contact with books, educational broadcasts, and computer programs, which were all devised by humans for the purpose of facilitating skill development or knowledge acquisition. Even though the authors of these educational aids are not physically present, they nonetheless in part control the learner's cognitive operations.

My own research into successful independent learning among adults of low educational attainment in the United Kingdom (Brookfield, 1982) showed that the adults whom I surveyed had placed their learning efforts very deliberately within a social context. These adults had all attained positions of local or national prominence (measured by the bestowal of peer acclaim) in their respective fields of interest. These fields were all avocational, and the adults concerned had developed their visibly high levels of expertise without the benefit of participation in formally planned programs of instruction. Hence, their activities were independent of sustained external instructional direction, independent of institutional accreditation, and independent of institutional financial support.

Despite these dimensions of independence, the learning activities of the adults whom I interviewed were placed consciously and deliberately within the context of informal learning networks. These networks and information exchanges provided evaluative indices for learning through peer comparison, and they established a setting within which the learners could act as skill models and resource consultants to fellow learners of varying levels of expertise.

Instead of using libraries, cassettes, and self-instructional programs, these adults chose to use peers, experts, and fellow learners as their chief sources of information and as their skill models. Their learning activities exemplify the oral tradition, whereby knowledge is transmitted from person to person in informal settings, despite the interest of this era in high technology and computer-aided learning. The exchange of information and the acquisition of skills necessary to the development of expertise were accomplished within a context of informal, oral educational transactions. Information was shared through spontaneous conversation, and those members of the network who were regarded as possessing outstanding talent in a particular area came to serve as skill models for enthusiasts possessing varying degrees of expertise. Thiel (1984) replicated this study in Quebec and found a similar reliance on learning networks among the adults whom he surveyed.

Self-Directed Learning and Learning Style

If we relate the notion of self-directed learning to cognitive styles, not to the location and use of external resources, then the concept that seems to hold the most promise for insight is the concept of field independence. Field-independent learners are characterized as analytical, socially independent, inner-directed, individualistic, and possessed of a strong sense of self-identity (Witkin, 1969). Such learners are presumed to be found most commonly in open, democratic societies, which emphasize self-control and autonomy. Field-dependent learners are deemed to be comfortable in highly regulated settings where norms are well defined and unchanging. Such learners are characteristically found in cultures that stress clear role definition, social control, strict upbringing of children, and respect for authority. As Pratt (1984, p. 151) comments, "a picture emerges of individuals with strong tendencies toward field dependence (FD) being less self-directed in their learning, wanting more structure and guidance from an instructor, and not preferring the independence that may be required in collaborative modes of education, unless there is sufficient structure and guidance provided."

The assumptions underlying the field independence–field dependence construct seem clear. Field independence is a learning style associated with open democracies, which encourage freedom and autonomy. Field dependence is characteristic of the learning conducted within rigidly controlled societies where adherence to imposed patterns of behavior and authoritarian control is valued above all else. To this extent, continuing educators who say that promotion of self-direction is the raison d'être of their efforts seem to favor a field-independent learning style. The single-mindedness, goal orientation, and planning capability of field independence is regarded as possessing more value than the field-dependent learner's awareness of context and external social orientation.

The work of Brookfield (1980, 1981, 1982) and Thiel (1984) forms an interesting empirical counterpoint to the field independence–field dependence construct. As Even (1982) points out, adult education philosophy appears to favor the self-directedness implicit in the field-independent learning style. However, the only two studies in the whole field of self-directed learning that have concentrated on the activities of successful independent learners — successful as measured by the relatively objective indicator of peer acclaim — report findings contrary to those that might be anticipated. Successful self-directed learners exhibit characteristics close to those of the field-dependent learning style in a number of significant ways. The learning activities of successful self-directed learners are placed within a social context, and other people are cited as the most important learning resource. Peers and fellow learners provide information, serve as skill models, and act as reinforcers of learning and as counselors at times of crisis. Successful self-directed learners appear to be highly aware of context in the sense that they place their learning within a social setting in which the advice, information, and skill modeling provided by other learners are crucial conditions for successful learning.

Self-Directed Learning and Independence

Although self-directed learning takes place in a social context, there is one sense in which we are all independent learners. As our nervous system receives information, stimuli, and messages, the mental strategies that we use to process, code, and internally classify these data assume an entirely idiosyncratic character. An adult's previous learning brings him or her to a particular mental equilibrium. That learning combines with the adult's past experiences to become a mediatory mechanism that classifies all new stimuli. Because all adult learners receive and codify stimuli in an individual and highly idiosyncratic manner, we can say that all learning exhibits some independence, whether that learning is institutionally sponsored or is conducted in informal settings. Such independence is manifest in the unique nature of each learner's mediatory mechanism.

The most commonly accepted definitions of self-teaching (Tough, 1967) and of self-directed learning (Knowles, 1975) emphasize the fact of the learner's control over the planning and execution of learning. Indeed, a strong measure of independence in controlling the direction and conduct of learning is taken as a defining feature of self-direction. However, it is dangerous to say that adults' independence must be marked by a highly regulated control over the purpose and intent of their activities if self-directed learning is to occur. Although some degree of direction and purpose is a necessary condition for any kind of education, it is possible for adults to embark on an intellectual quest with no closely specified, fixed, or terminal point in mind. Indeed, many adults engaged in purposeful learning do not specify the skills or knowledge that they are attempting to acquire. An adult can embark on independent exploration of a field of knowledge with no real idea of how to design learning activities that will result in the development of a certain level of proficiency. It is only as the adult becomes aware of the standards, operations, procedures, and criteria deemed intrinsic to that skill or knowledge area that he or she can begin to set short- and long-term learning goals.

It is possible to apply the techniques of self-directed learning in a number of contexts for different purposes. These techniques are more or less context-free. We can become self-directed in a technical, mechanistic sense (in terms of setting goals, locating resources, implementing strategies, and evaluating progress) in such diverse activities as learning to ride a bike, becoming skilled in playing the guitar, developing an appreciation of the work of Mozart, broadening our knowledge of the Middle Eastern political situation, or learning about political theory. However, in all the examples just cited, the conduct of a self-directed learning project can be placed within a predefined framework. We operate within self-imposed limits, and to this extent we are trapped in our own history. It is hard to imagine an adult deciding to shift paradigms, transform perspectives, or replace one meaning system with another purely as a result of his or her own free will. How can adults conceive of alternative ways of interpreting the world or of recreating their personal and collective circumstances if they are not helped to realize that there are other states of being? One task of the adult teacher, therefore, is to encourage adult students to view knowledge and truth as contextual, to see value frameworks as cultural constructs, and to appreciate that they can act on their world individually or collectively and that they can transform it. In assisting adults to realize their adulthood by coming to appreciate their power to transform their personal and collective worlds lies the unique mission of the adult educator. Jack Mezirow discusses this mission in Chapter Two.

Self-Directed Learners and Middle-Class Life-Styles

The middle-class nature of the majority of samples selected to represent the research universe for investigations of self-directed learning is one of the most consistent features of this research. The initial study of self-teachers conducted by Tough (1967) was comprised of interviews with forty college graduates in Toronto. The samples for his later studies (1968, 1979, 1982) have been drawn primarily from educationally advantaged populations. The groups surveyed by other researchers have typically been drawn from a similarly class-specific sampling frame. Hence, we have surveys of professional men, pharmacists, teachers, parish ministers, clergy, graduate students, degreed engineers, and nurses. Brookfield (1983) discusses these studies in detail.

It is evident, then, that the resultant generalizations will be culture-and class-specific. We certainly cannot claim that the groups investigated are statistically representative of the total American or Canadian population. The great majority of individuals in these groups have attained an educational level that is above the average. To assume that the behaviors of these educationally advantaged adults will be displayed by adults from different class and ethnic backgrounds is unjustified.

Indeed, to base talk of a specifically adult propensity for self-directed learning on research into samples comprised chiefly of white, middle-class Americans is dangerously ethnocentric. Very few researchers have chosen to investigate the self-directed learning activities of working-class adults in America. Armstrong (1971), Johnson and others (1977), and Leann and Sisco (1981) have conducted studies with such groups, while Elsey (1974) and Brookfield (1980) have researched the use made of informal learning networks in self-directed learning by adults of low educational attainment in England. Compared with the catalogue of investigations of educationally advantaged populations outlined earlier, such studies are few indeed.

Also conspicuous by their absence are cross-cultural studies of self-directed learning among blacks, Puerto Ricans, Hispanics, Asians, or native Americans. The creation of informal networks and the fostering of self-directedness among immigrant cultures, such as the Chinese, would seem to offer fascinating material for intercultural analysis of self-directedness. To build a theory of self-directed learning on the studies cited earlier and to claim that such a theory represents a uniquely adult domain of learning theory is to balance an inverted pyramid of concepts and theoretical generalizations on the apex of a highly class- and culture-specific group of studies. Studies of self-directedness in other classes and cultures may cause this theoretical edifice to topple, but it will prevent us from accepting uncritically broad concepts of adult learning derived from a dangerously narrow sampling frame.

Methods of Investigation in Self-Directed Learning

In a provocative essay, Alvin Gouldner (1967) coined the term *methodolatry* to describe the process by which researchers develop a slavish and uncritical adherence to a particular research mode irrespective of the success of that mode in producing new knowledge or in suggesting new concepts and hypotheses. The most serious consequence of a methodolatrous subscription to certain research techniques is its effect on the framing and conduct of research. The criteria by which we judge whether questions are important enough to research become the extent to which these topics can be investigated with a certain methodology. Thus, our definition of a problem as important, relevant, or profound becomes a statement about the phenomena, events, or behaviors that are susceptible of investigation through a particular methodology. Instead of framing a research problem as one to be investigated on its own merits because it is significant, researchers assign significance to a problem according to whether it is amenable to investigation within the dominant methodological paradigm of the day.

Research into self-directed learning has been methodolatrous in the commitment of researchers to structured interview schedules, questionnaires, prompt sheets, and measurement scales. The majority of studies in this area administer a modified version of the schedules, prompt sheets, and questionnaires devised by Tough and his team. More recently, the Self-Directed Learning Readiness Scale (SDLRS) devised by Guglielmino (1977) has prompted a new wave of dissertations.

This emphasis on quasi-quantitative instruments has several consequences. The first involves the way in which such instruments become self-defining regarding the learning activities that they uncover. If the researcher seeks unequivocal, quantitative measures of learning, it is likely that subjects will, perhaps unwittingly, concentrate on recalling learning projects that appear to meet the expectations reflected in the researcher's methodology. Hence, the finding that learning projects most commonly originate in the assignment to learners of an action goal (Tough, 1968), usually of a vocational nature, may be the result of a tendency among researchers to present examples of easily identified psychomotor skills projects when discussing "typical" learning projects with their subjects at the outset of an interview. It is much easier for an adult to recall the assistants consulted, the time spent, the goal-setting procedure used, and the nonhuman materials that were the most helpful if the individual is describing the process by which he or she repaired a car or rewired a basement. External, behavioral indexes of learning—number of hours spent, number of assistants consulted, number of books read—become much harder to obtain and more ambiguous in nature if we seek, for example, to explore the individual's development of esthetic appreciation, the raising of an individual's political consciousness, or the development of interpersonal sensitivity.

A second consequence of the adoption of formalized measures of self-directed learning, interview protocols, and self-administered questionnaires is that such investigative hardware can intimidate learners. Working-class adults and members of ethnic minorities or recently arrived immigrant groups are likely to be suspicious of batteries of scales, prompt sheets, and questionnaires, which they associate with the world of welfare officialdom. Also, as Brockett (1984) has pointed out, the SDLRS is suited to measuring the readiness for self-directed learning of adults who have an average or above-average level of formal educational attainment and who rely on books and periodicals for information. With adults of little formal education or with adults who have used fellow learners as the primary source of information in their explorations of knowledge and skill areas, the SDLRS is a questionable measure of readiness for learning.

Studies of self-directed learning have generally relied on structured interview schedules and precoded categories of response that subjects' perceptions of their learning are made to fit. Lists of self-directed learning projects, definitions of major learning efforts, lists of individuals typically assisting in the conduct of self-directed learning, lists of reasons for starting learning projects, various prompt sheets—all these have been presented to self-directed learners in an attempt to elicit information about learning efforts.

Using such standardized instruments with groups of working-class adults or with learners from certain ethnic minorities will cause these individuals to regard the researcher with suspicion. Suspicion is not likely to foster the trust and reciprocity that are necessary to an authentic research encounter, in which the subject states as truthfully and accurately as possible the details concerning the planning and execution of a learning project.

A third result of the application of strictly defined and tightly administered quantitative measures in the investigation of self-directed learning is that the quality of such learning is overlooked. Although there has been an understandable desire to estimate the number of hours that adults spend conducting their own learning, there has not been a comparable attention to the quality or effectiveness of that learning. Relying solely on self-reported estimations concerning the success and quality of learning is clearly questionable. Just as self-assigned measures of social class tend to reflect adults' desire to place themselves in a higher category than the one to which they would objectively be assigned, so learners are likely to claim for their efforts a degree of effectiveness that external, objective assessment might not confirm. A crucial area for further research, therefore, is the congruence or disjunction between adults' own judgments regarding the quality of their learning and that quality as measured by some external, objective standard.

Finally, the literature on self-directed learning does not deal with the innate worth or value of individual learning activities. Research designs in this area tend to treat all learning projects as possessing equal significance for the learner. However, it is evident that individual projects are very different in their internal characteristics, in their personal meaning to the adult concerned, and in their significance for society at large. To compare learning to deal with divorce or bereavement with learning to wire a basement or repair a car is methodologically unsound. It is comparing like with unlike. The only commonality lies in the fact that the learner controls the planning and conduct of a majority of learning activities. To assume that these different learning activities are conceptually or substantively equivalent because they exhibit some similarities of technique is clearly absurd.

Self-Directed Learning and the Realization of Adulthood

In their analyses of autonomy in learning, Strong (1977) and Chené (1983) argue that autonomy cannot simply be equated with learner control over goals and methods of learning. These authors assert that truly autonomous learning can occur only when learners have full knowledge of the possible alternative learning activities. In the next chapter, Mezirow explores the same issue. The point made by all three writers is an important one: It is simplistic for us to conceive of self-direction solely in terms of command of self-instructional techniques. To do so means that we can speak of self-directed learners operating within fixed and uncritically assimilated frameworks of knowledge. From this viewpoint, it is possible to be a superb technician of self-directed learning, as measured by one's command of goal-setting, instructional design, or evaluative procedures, and yet never to ask whether one's intellectual pursuit is valid or worthwhile or never to compare it with competing, alternative possibilities. According to this argument, one can speak quite seriously of a self-directed party member or of a self-directed religious zealot who is completely unaware of alternative political doctrines or religious creeds. It is enough for the learner to be skilled in certain technical activities concerned with the design and management of self-instruction.

The concept of self-directed learning advanced in this chapter diverges sharply from this technicist perspective. It assumes a more constructivist, sociopolitical character, and it should be understood in the context of the critical philosophy outlined in the next chapter. At its heart is the notion of autonomy — an understanding and awareness of a range of alternative possibilities — as advanced both by Strong (1977) and by Chené (1983). Hence, self-directed learning is predicated on adults' awareness of their separateness and on their consciousness of their personal power. When they come to view their personal and social worlds as contingent and therefore accessible to individual and collective interventions, then the internal disposition necessary for self-directed action exists. When adults take action to acquire skills and knowledge in order to effect these interventions, then they are exemplifying principles of self-directed learning. They are realizing their autonomy in the act of learning, and they are investing that act with a sense of personal meaning.

It becomes clear that in future discussion of the concept of self-direction as the characteristic feature of adult learning, we should distinguish between the techniques of self-direction and the internal change in consciousness that we can call *self-directed learning*. The technique of self-directed learning is manifest in the individual's ability to plan and conduct learning activities. It is discernible when the individual sets realistic and achievable objectives, locates and chooses appropriate resources, designs learning strategies, and generates evaluative procedures. Such activities are primarily mechanistic in that the learner is concerned with perfecting technique in order to achieve specified goals as quickly and as efficiently as possible. It is quite feasible, then, to exhibit the methodological attributes of self-directed learning within a framework of assumptions, expectations, allowable goals, and possible alternatives that is narrow and unchallenged. Learning to be a good disciple, an efficient bureaucratic functionary, or an exemplary political party member are all projects where the techniques of self-directed learning are evident. At the same time, none of these projects exhibits autonomous critical thought concerning alternatives, options, or possibilities.

As the mode of learning characteristic of adults who are in the process of realizing their adulthood, self-directed learning is concerned much more with an internal change of consciousness than with the external management of instructional events. This consciousness involves an appreciation of the contextuality of knowledge and an awareness of the culturally constructed form of value frameworks, belief systems, and moral codes that influence behavior and the creation of social structures. The most complete form of self-directed learning occurs when process and reflection are married in the adult's pursuit of meaning. As just noted, it is possible to show that one is a technically skilled self-directed learner in one's attempt to be a good party member, employee, or graduate student. The norms or assumptions underlying what it means to be good in any of these settings never need to be questioned. The only thing that is required for an activity to be a technically correct example of self-directed learning is for the individual concerned to be effective in designing a successful learning program with a minimum of external assistance.

When the techniques of self-directed learning are allied with the adult's quest for critical reflection and the creation of personal meaning after due consideration of a full range of alternative value frameworks and action possibilites, then the most complete form of self-directed learning is exemplified. This most fully adult form of self-directed learning is one in which critical reflection on the contextual and contingent aspects of reality, the exploration of alternative perspectives and meaning systems, and the alteration of personal and social circumstances are all present. The external technical dimension is fused with the internal, reflective dimension when adults come to appreciate the culturally constructed nature of knowledge and values and when they act on the basis of that appreciation to reinterpret and recreate their personal and social worlds. In such a praxis of thought and action is manifested a fully adult form of autonomous, self-directed learning.

References

Armstrong, D. "Adult Learners of Low Educational Attainment: The Self-Concepts, Backgrounds, and Educative Behavior of Average- and High-Learning Adults of Low Educational Attainment." Unpublished doctoral dissertation, University of Toronto, 1971.

Brockett, R. "Methodological and Substantive Issues in the Measurement of Self-Directed Learning Readiness." Paper presented at the Adult Education Research Conference, Raleigh, N.C., April 1984.

Brookfield, S. "Independent Adult Learning." Unpublished doctoral dissertation, University of Leicester, 1980.

Brookfield, S. "Independent Adult Learning." *Studies in Adult Education,* 1981, *13* (1), 15–27.

Brookfield, S. "The Parallel Educational Universe: Successful Independent Learning of Adults of Low Educational Attainment in the United Kingdom." Paper presented at the Adult Education Research Conference, Lincoln, Neb., April 1982.

Brookfield, S. *Adult Learners, Adult Education, and the Community.* New York: Teachers College Press, 1983.

Chené, A. "The Concept of Autonomy in Adult Education: A Philosophical Discussion." *Adult Education Quarterly,* 1983, *34* (1), 38–47.

Elsey, B. "Voluntary Organization and Informal Adult Education." *Adult Education,* (U.K.), 1974, *46* (6), 391–396.

Even, M. J. "Adapting Cognitive Style Theory in Practice." *Lifelong Learning: The Adult Years,* 1982, *5* (5), 14–16, 27.

Farquharson, A. "Peers as Helpers: Personal Change in Members of Self-Help Groups in Metropolitan Toronto." Unpublished doctoral dissertation, University of Toronto, 1975.

Gouldner, A. *Enter Plato.* London: Routledge & Kegan Paul, 1967.

Guglielmino, L. M. "Development of the Self-Directed Learning Readiness Scale." Unpublished doctoral dissertation, University of Georgia, 1977.

Johnson, V., Levine, H., and Rosenthal, E. L. *Learning Projects of Unemployed Adults in New Jersey.* New Brunswick, N.J.: Educational Advancement Project, Rutgers Labor Education Center, 1977.

Knowles, M. S. *Self-Directed Learning: A Guide for Learners and Teachers.* New York: Cambridge Book, 1975.

Leann, C., and Sisco, B. *Learning Projects and Self-Planned Learning Efforts Among Undereducated Adults in Rural Vermont.* Washington, D.C.: National Institute of Education, 1981.

Moore, M. G. "Towards a Theory of Independent Learning." *Journal of Higher Education,* 1973, *44* (12), 661–679.

Pratt, D. "Andragogical Assumptions: Some Counterintuitive Logic." Paper presented at the Adult Education Research Conference, Raleigh, N.C., April 1984.

Strong, M. "The Autonomous Adult Learner." Unpublished master's of education thesis, University of Nottingham, 1977.

Thiel, J. P. "Successful Self-Directed Learners' Learning Styles." Paper presented at the Adult Education Research Conference, Raleigh, N.C., April 1984.

Tough, A. M. *Learning Without a Teacher.* Toronto: Ontario Institute for Studies in Education, 1967.

Tough, A. M. *Why Adults Learn.* Toronto: Ontario Institute for Studies in Education, 1968.

Tough, A. M. *The Adult's Learning Projects: A Fresh Approach to Theory and Practice in Adult Learning.* (2nd ed.) Austin, Texas: Learning Concepts, 1979.

Tough, A. M. *Intentional Changes.* Chicago: Follett, 1982.

Witkin, H. A. "Social Influences in the Development of Cognitive Style." In D. A. Goslin (Ed.), *Handbook of Socialization Theory and Research.* New York: Rand McNally, 1969.

Stephen Brookfield is assistant professor of adult and continuing education and associate director of the Center for Adult Education at Teachers College, Columbia University, New York City.

Becoming critically aware of what has been taken for granted about
one's own learning is the key to self-directedness.

A Critical Theory of
Self-Directed Learning

Jack Mezirow

No concept is more central to what adult education is all about than self-directed learning. An adult has been defined as one who fulfills adult social roles and who sees himself or herself as a self-directed person. Malcolm Knowles (1975, p. 18) describes self-directed learning as "a process in which individuals take the initiative without the help of others in diagnosing their learning needs, formulating goals, identifying human and material resources, and evaluating learning outcomes." Self-directed learning is the goal of andragogy, the prevailing philosophy of adult education, an orientation "aimed at enabling people to become aware that they should be the originators of their thinking and feeling" (Nottingham Andragogy Group, 1983, p. 2). This chapter speculates on the purposes, processes, and conditions required for learning aimed at such awareness; it critically analyzes some commonly held assumptions; and it suggests the implications for adult educators.

In essence, the purpose of learning is to enable us to understand the meaning of our experiences and to realize values in our lives. For the most part, we learn new meanings by spelling out an experience or an aspect of an experience that we have not yet made explicit and by seeking to validate our interpretation of its meanings.

To understand self-directed learning, it may be useful to differentiate three interrelated but distinct functions of adult learning: instrumental

S. Brookfield (Ed.). *Self-Directed Learning: From Theory to Practice.* New Directions
for Continuing Education, no. 25. San Francisco: Jossey-Bass, March 1985.

learning—task-oriented problem solving that is relevant for controlling the environment or other people; dialogic learning, by which we attempt to understand what others mean in communicating with us; and self-reflective learning, by which we come to understand ourselves (Mezirow, 1981). Each function has its own distinctive learning purpose, content, and methods and its own criteria for assessing the validity of an idea (Habermas, 1971). It follows that such differences extend both to the needs of self-directed learners and to appropriate educational approaches.

Instrumental Learning

When an experience involves the world of facts, we can determine the truth of an idea empirically. John Dewey and the pragmatists showed us how instrumental learning is an analogue of the research methods used in the natural sciences. One responds to a problematic situation by formulating hypothetical courses of action, anticipating the consequences of each, selecting the most plausible, and testing its validity by acting on it and assessing the results. Generalizations are deduced from hypotheses. Piaget described this form of reasoning in terms of formal operations.

In instrumental learning, meaning is inferred deductively: One tests a hypothetical meaning scheme that one believes will influence a cause–effect relationship in a way that increases control over a problematic situation. To hit a golf ball so that it will land close to the hole (cause–effect), one analyzes the variables—both those that have to do with style and technique and those that have to do with conditions of distance, wind, and terrain. If past experience gives us reason to believe that we can increase our control by changing the way in which we hold the club, we can test this hypothesis by holding the other variables constant and alternating our grip on the club. If the resulting swing places the ball closer to the hole than we have been able to place it before, we take the hypothesis to be true.

This kind of learning always involves a prediction about observable things or events that can be proved correct or incorrect. A proposition can be established as valid by demonstrating its empirical truth and the correctness of the analyses involved. A statement is true if it corresponds to observed experience. Problem solving involves the analysis of variables, the breaking of a whole situation up into its parts. Learning is directed toward determination of cause–effect relationships. The knowledge gained is prescriptive. Action is instrumental in nature, involving attempts to increase one's control in order to increase one's success in performance. Effective control is the criterion that we use to judge what action is appropriate. Instrumental learning is learning how to; it does not deal with why.

Perhaps the most pervasive distortion in the field of continuing education results from our assumption that all adult learning proceeds exactly as instrumental learning does. This fallacy of misplaced concreteness has anesthetized educators to the other major functions of learning, and it has obscured the appropriate uses of education and the appropriate research methods for each.

Dialogic Learning

Most significant learning in adulthood involves moral issues; ideals; values; abstract social, political, philosophical, or educational concepts; and feelings. We attempt to learn what others mean as they communicate with us through speech, the written word, plays, moving pictures, television, and art. Symbolic interaction involves assertions about the meaning of a vast range of experience in several dimensions, ranging from the concrete to the abstract and poetic. We must interpret the meaning of these assertions without the benefit of an empirical method for establishing objectively the validity of what is right or wrong, correct or incorrect. And yet, in everyday speech we are continually confronted with having to determine the validity of reports, predictions, explanations, arguments, and denials as well as the implicit claims of validity involved in justifying commands, requests, excuses, and recommendations.

In the absence of empirical tests, we learn what is valid in the assertions of others, and we gain credence for the validity of our own ideas by relying on as broad a consensus as possible of those whom we accept as informed, objective, and rational. Because new information and new criteria of rationality can always emerge, the validity of consensual judgments arrived at through dialogue is always provisional.

Usually, we take for granted that what is said to us by others meets four criteria: It is comprehensible, it is true, the speaker is truthful or sincere, and what is asserted is appropriate to the situation (McCarthy, 1979). On those pivotal occasions when any of these four conditions appears questionable, dialogue is sidetracked until the issue is resolved. It is at these junctures in our experience that dialogic learning takes on a critical new dimension. We enter into a reflective assessment of validity that the philosopher Jurgen Habermas (1971) calls _discourse_. Complete understanding is often predicated on a critical questioning of the assumptions on which the prevailing norms of appropriateness are based.

Ideally, participants in a discourse have full information about the matter at issue, they are able to reason argumentatively, they can reflect critically about assumptions and premises, and they have sufficient self-knowledge to assure that participation in discourse is free of self-deception. Participants in such discourse are free of constraint or coercion, and they enjoy full equality and reciprocity in assuming the various roles involved in the discourse. The resulting consensus is based on the cogency of argument alone. While historical, hierarchical, ideological, institutional, and psychological restraints distort the process of discourse in everyday life, these idealized conditions are implicit in the very nature of human communication. They provide valuable criteria for judging the conditions of dialogic learning and for fostering self-direction.

Ideal here is used not in the sense of unattainable perfection but as a judgment of value that is implicit in all dialogue and in our educational efforts to facilitate it, much as we use the ideal of self-directed learning in everyday educational parlance. As John Walker Powell (1956, p. 231) observed nearly three decades ago in an analysis of how continuing educators can derive the values of their profession from an understanding of the critical function of human communication, "The ideal is *present* in every act, as a judgment of better and worse."

The learning method of dialogic learning appears to be less one of testing hypotheses than one of analyzing a phenomenon and drawing metaphorically on elements in an existing meaning scheme to devise a parallel set of concepts for construing the phenomenon. In this way, some metaphors can permit us to see aspects of reality that they themselves help to constitute. For example, when labor is metaphorically interpreted as a substance, like a natural resource, it can then be quantified, be assigned a value per unit of quantity, serve a purpose, and be progressively used up as it serves that purpose (Lakoff and Johnson, 1980). The view of labor as an activity implies that a clear distinction can be made between work and play and between productive and nonproductive labor. These are not easy distinctions most of the time. Viewing labor as mere activity — independent of who performs it, of how it is experienced, and of its meaning in one's life — separates the concept of work from issues of whether it is personally meaningful or satisfying and from its role in identity development and recreative realization. Metaphors should be understood first as matters of thought and action and only secondarily as a matter of language. Lakoff and Johnson (1980) point out that such concepts as labor, love, health, time, happiness, understanding, and morality require metaphorical definition.

In dialogic learning, knowledge is designative rather than prescriptive. Through dialectical reasoning and argumentation, consensual judgments become possible. The purpose of dialogic learning is not to establish cause-effect relationships but to increase insight and understanding through symbolic interaction. Action is communicative rather than instrumental. The type of inference involved is called *abductive;* abductive inference yields a tentative explanation. The learner draws on his or her experience to explain, and that process suggests what to look for next. Hanson (1981, p. 69) succinctly explains, "Deduction proves something *must* be. Induction shows that something actually is operative. Abduction suggests that something *may* be."

Self-Reflective Learning

Self-reflective learning focuses on gaining a clearer understanding of oneself by identifying dependency-producing psychological assumptions acquired earlier in life that have become dysfunctional in adulthood. They have come to impede the kind of life that the learner wishes to live as an adult.

The process of socialization makes us all heir to such distorting assumptions. Traumatic childhood events can cause us to learn specific prohibitions — never confront, never succeed, never express feelings, never be the center of attention, never do less than better than others, and so forth. The inhibitory rule fades from consciousness, but it continues into adulthood to influence behavior. The way it influences behavior is by evoking feelings of anxiety when adult action threatens to violate the prohibition. The distorting and dependence–producing assumption is that violating the rule will produce the calamitous consequences most feared by the traumatized child — complete loss of control, death or violence to a parent, public humiliation, total rejection, and so forth. This assumption is unwarranted by one's adult situation. The learning involved brings such restrictive psychological assumptions into consciousness and initiates an internal dialogue that differentiates the past and our anxiety symptoms from the realities of our adult present. Only then can we come to understand the meaning of these feelings and impulses and of dysfunctional patterns for dealing with rejection and take corrective action to overcome them.

Psychoanalytic therapy has played a central role in self-reflective learning. However, adult educators need to be able to facilitate this important learning function and increase their sophistication in the dynamics of psychoeducational practice, particularly as it pertains to the existential dilemmas generated by such common life transitions as the death of a mate or child, divorce, change in job status or being passed over for promotion, retirement, mid-career burnout, and others.

Knowledge gained through self-reflective learning is appraisive rather than prescriptive or designative. Action is emancipatory. The learner is presented with an alternative way of interpreting feelings and patterns of action; the old meaning scheme or perspective is reorganized to incorporate new insights; we come to see our reality more inclusively, to understand it more clearly, and to integrate our experience better. Only the individual involved can determine the validity of the reorganized meaning scheme or perspective. A coherence theory is relevant here. Coherence theory holds that the more valid a meaning scheme or perspective the more closely will the facts it addresses be related, and the more will it organize and bring together.

Meaning Schemes and Perspectives

Meaning perspective refers to the structure of cultural and psychological assumptions within which our past experience assimilates and transforms new experience. It is a frame of reference made up from a system of meaning schemes. Meaning schemes are sets of related expectations governing cause-effect relationships (blow in my ear, and I'll follow you anywhere), roles (teacher, student), social action (democratic activists, radical agitators), ourselves (masculine macho, mother and homemaker), values (bad, good, ugly, beautiful, right, wrong), and making connections between feelings and action (avoid all confrontation, or you will become violent). They guide the way in which we experience, feel, understand, judge, and act upon our situation. A meaning perspective is a personal paradigm involving cognitive, conative, and affective dimensions. It positions us for action. By defining our expectations, it also selectively orders what we learn and the way we learn it.

However serendipitous, limited, or untrustworthy the uncritically assimilated meaning schemes and perspectives that we acquire in childhood and youth may be, adulthood gives us an opportunity for reappraisal and corrective action. Developmentally, adults can acquire a new capability for critical reflection and a new mode of interpreting reality through a heightened awareness of the relevance of context.

When a meaning perspective increases participation in the process of constructing meaning through dialogue, it can be considered a more authentic and more valid meaning perspective. Thus, one meaning perspective is more authentic than another meaning perspective when it is more informed by complete and accurate information; more inclusive, discriminating, and integrative of experience; more free from the influence of internal or external constraint or coercion; more critically reflective—informed by a clear understanding of the historical, cultural, and biographical reasons for its having been acquired in the first place and of the functions that it fulfills; and more permeable—open to discourse with alternative perspectives on disputed validity claims.

Perspective transformation refers to the process of becoming critically aware of how and why the structure of our psychocultural assumptions has come to constrain the way in which we perceive our world, of reconstituting that structure in a way that allows us to be more inclusive and discriminating in our integration of experience and to act on these new understandings (Mezirow, 1975, 1978). Perspective transformation is the process by which adults come to recognize introjected dependency roles and relationships and the reasons for them and to take action to overcome them.

We move toward more authentic meaning perspectives when our culture and circumstances permit, because more authentic meaning perspectives provide us with a clearer understanding of the meaning of our experience. The fully functioning, self-directed, adult learner moves consistently toward a more authentic meaning perspective.

Learning Processes

Three learning processes are operative in each of the domains involving instrumental, dialogic, and self-reflective learning functions. The processes are somewhat similar to those described by Bateson (1972). The first process is learning within meaning schemes—learning to further differentiate and elaborate the acquired meaning schemes that we take for granted, learning within the structure of our acquired frames of reference. For example, instrumentally, we learn that we must keep our head down as we swing a golf club if we want to improve our drive; dialogically, we learn that *honesty* can refer to self-disclosure as well as to abiding by the law; self-reflectively, we learn the limits of our tolerance of ambiguity.

This process of learning includes habitual and stereotypic responses to information received through preexisting, known categories of meaning — what has been described as "recipe learning" — as well as rote learning, in which one behavior is the stimulus to another behavior. One can become aware of context markers, but the context (meaning scheme) does not change. The only thing that changes by correction of errors within a meaning scheme is the specificity of response.

(2) The second process is learning new meaning schemes — arguing new meaning schemes that are sufficiently consistent and compatible with existing meaning schemes to complement them within a prevailing meaning perspective. Instrumentally, we learn to take tests; dialogically, we learn the meaning of a learning theory, or we learn to play a new role; self-reflectively, we learn to think of ourselves in terms of a new classification, such as introverted, or we discover that we are inhibited in some area of experiencing.

In this process of learning, context — in the form of either related meaning schemes or perspective — does not change. The prevailing perspective is strengthened, because the understanding that it makes possible extends to new areas of experience. In this process of learning, meaning schemes may be assimilated consciously or unself-consciously in the course of socialization. Identification plays a large role in this kind of learning.

(3) The third process is learning through meaning transformation — becoming aware of specific assumptions (schemata, criteria, rules, or repressions) on which a distorted or incomplete meaning scheme is based and, through a reorganization of meaning, transforming it. We encounter a patch of meaninglessness or an anomaly that cannot be given coherence either by learning within a meaning scheme or by learning complementary new meaning schemes. Illumination comes only through a redefinition of the problem. Redefinition is achieved by critically reassessing the assumptions that support the meaning scheme in use.

A transformation can involve either a particular meaning scheme or a cluster, set, or structure of meaning schemes, that is, a meaning perspective. A specific false assumption can be recognized and changed. A chair that appears to be stationary is understood to be moving because the earth is rotating, or one recognizes his or her use of a stereotype or one's false childhood assumption that, if one confronts, one will lose control and become violent. Similarly, the structure of assumptions (belief system, ideology, or paradigm) is brought into consciousness and negated in favor of an alternative perspective, or a synthesis is effected to reconcile elements of the old and the new ways of seeing.

Through instrumental learning, an urban planner may come to negate or modify a metaphorical assumption that causes a slum to be seen as a blighted community that can be restored to health only by removing dilapidated buildings and by designing new environments in favor of an alternative metaphorical view of the slum as a natural community. The second viewpoint places the emphasis on social integration, homelike stability, and informal networks of mutual support to be preserved and strengthened through aided self-help (Schon, 1979).

Through dialogic learning in the form of conscientization, a peasant can come to understand how his whole lifetime of relationships with a patron or zamindar has been based on an oppressive and unwarranted dependency (Freire, 1970). Through consciousness raising, a woman can come to see how her old belief system was predicated on sex-stereotypic thinking and reject it as oppressive. Dialogic learning enables one to recognize that distorting assumptions or ideologies that one has taken for granted often touch on one's self-concept. This can lead to self-reflective learning if one attempts to understand how and why he or she has come to internalize these distortions in the first place.

In self-reflective learning, we recognize a pattern of behavior governed by feelings of anxiety generated by repressed parental prohibition — never confront, never do less than best, never be sensual — or by feelings and actions associated with rejection and by the games that we play to make the pattern of behavior appear more congruent with the way we would like to be as adults. This is the kind of learning that takes place in psychotherapy through transference; it is a new way of seeing old ways of being.

These are the ways in which transformation works: Old meaning schemes or perspectives are brought into consciousness and negated, or they are modified and synthesized with a more insightful new viewpoint. One learns propositions about meaning schemas and perspectives, habits of gestalt perception become modified, contexts change, and premises shift.

Perspective transformation occurs in two dimensions, either through an accretion of transformations in specific meaning schemes or as an epochal transformation of a system of meaning schemes. The former is more common, the latter more dramatic. Epochal transformations involving a belief system or ideology are well known in conscientization, consciousness raising, psychoanalysis, Zen experience, and religious conversion. Bateson (1972, p. 231) characterizes the learning that goes on in epochal transformations as "discovery that all pain and joy of fitting one's self into the perceived world was premised upon personal perceptions of the world." Such learning is painful, because it often involves a comprehensive reassessment of oneself and the very criteria that one has been using to make crucial value judgments about one's life. In transformations in dialogic learning and particularly in self-reflective learning, which makes self-concept so central, the affective dimension of learning plays a critical role. Learning to understand the meaning of one's feelings and to take action, despite the fears and impulses now seen as irrational, is not easy, especially when existing social norms strongly disapprove. Learning by transformation can be aborted if one intellectualizes a new point of view without learning to deal with the strong feelings that accompany it. It can also be aborted by mindless identification with a new group or belief system, which relieves one's feelings of ambiguity at the expense of critical reflectivity and openness to new alternative perspectives. This is why we need to make a distinction between switching our identification to others or a new belief system and contractual solidarity, by which we enter into new commitments after critical reflection and with explicit conditions for maintaining allegiance. A self-directed learner's commitment to a belief system is predicated on contractual solidarity, a solidarity that does not limit dialogue but enables one to participate more fully in an expanded dialogue.

Reflectivity and Context in Adult Learning

The possibilities of learning through transformations in meaning schemes and perspectives become qualitatively different in the adult years, when we move from an awareness of the conceptual and psychic constraints on our learning toward an understanding of the reasons for these constraints.

With the advent in adolescence of a hypothetical-deductive mode of thought — Piaget's stage of formal operation — rules become seen in the broad context of governing principles (why should I do it?), and they are challenged when they seem to be incongruent with the new context. In adulthood, the reasons for principles are more likely to be sought through critical examination of broad paradigmatic (instrumental learning), ideological (dialogic learning), or psychodynamic (self-reflective learning) contexts. As we age, we can become more attentive to context and more critically reflective of meanings taken for granted that at an earlier age we perceived as context-independent.

As adults, we may arrive at truly dialectical meaning perspectives, in which acts and events are understood not as they appear at the moment but as they appear in the context of their history, the direction and pace of their developmental growth, and their probable consequences on the lives of those affected. Principles become less standards of judgment and more rules of thumb for the interpretation of situations in context. Perhaps a fully mature self-directed learner would make moral decisions from such a meaning perspective.

The most egregious and inexplicable omission from the literature of adult learning theory is the uniquely adult function of critical reflectivity, which is what makes meaning transformations possible. The prevailing concept of reflective thinking is limited to the interpretation of data, application of fact and principles, and logical reasoning (Knowles, 1975). Gagne's (1972) delineation of types of learning confines higher-order functions to application of principles and problem solving. As we have seen, critical reflectivity — the bringing of one's assumptions, premises, criteria, and schemata into consciousness and vigorously critiquing them — is indispensible in self-reflective learning, essential in dialogic learning, and significant in instrumental learning. In Mezirow's (1981) analysis, the levels of critical reflectivity include conceptual reflectivity (I am using a stereotype), psychic reflectivity (I am afraid to confront), and theoretical reflectivity (why am I using a stereotype, or why am I afraid to confront? What are the reasons for these actions or feelings?).

Learning Needs

By definition, the self-directed learner diagnoses his or her own learning needs and formulates his or her own learning goals. If the self-directed learner is fully functioning, he or she would do this for instrumental, dialogic, and self-directed learning, which all are more or less involved in most situations.

Knowles (1975) delineates a three-step self-diagnostic process. First, develop a model of desired behaviors or required competencies. Next, assess the present level of performance in each behavior and competence. Finally, assess the gaps between the model and the present performance. This process yields a dependable assessment of learning needs.

While specifying in advance the specific performance competencies to be acquired may have relevance for some aspects of instrumental learning, such a formulation seems to have little to offer when one is concerned with trying to understand what others mean or to learn about oneself. As we have seen, these functions of learning have purposes other than improving performance.

Even in instrumental learning, this approach has limited applicability. When a job requires proficiency in manual or highly technical skills with which the learner is unfamiliar, it seems inappropriate to expect the learner to take the initiative in planning, carrying out, and evaluating the learning experience. The irony is that it is precisely this kind of learning that is most amenable to specification of the required competencies as skills to be acquired so that learning gains can be measured in terms of increased levels of demonstrated competence. The learner cannot know what his or her learning needs are when he or she does not know what is required to become a machinist, build a bridge, or perform a root canal operation. The same thing is true when the subject matter to be learned is hierarchical and observes an ordered progression, as in the case of algebra, where beginning algebra precedes advanced algebra. A learner would know his or her learning needs if he or she could know what he or she could want. Obviously, there are many areas of learning where self-directedness as Knowles defines it does not apply.

One may put together a list of desired competencies and frame them as objectives involving learning within existing meaning schemes or learning new meaning schemes, but at significant junctures instrumental learning will involve critical reflectivity and meaning transformation. These processes are essential to full participation in dialogic learning, and they are central to self-reflective learning. Because meaning transformation involves a redefinition of the learning problem and the learner's interests, the direction of learning is in ascending spirals rather than linear; one goes back in order to go forward.

Perception and goals are always consistent with a world view or system of values and priorities—a perspective—that guides thought and action. It is not always feasible to formulate goals in advance in terms that the learner will understand, because the understanding comes only through the new structures—cognitive, conative, and affective—that will be learned.

There is probably no such thing as a self-directed learner, except in the sense that there is a learner who can participate fully and freely in the dialogue through which we test our interests and perspectives against those of others and accordingly modify them and our learning goals. Inasmuch as all other ideas and ideals in life are amenable to modification through experience, it seems gratuitous to fix learning objectives at the outset as criteria against which learning gains are to be assessed.

There are other problems. Adults often are not fully aware of their own best interests. A person can say that he or she wants something, but the statement may not be consistent with his or her action. An adult can also act in a way that clearly reflects needs of which the person is unaware. The ultimate criterion for determining whether a desire is an interest that should be satisfied is some ideal conception of the way in which one wants to live as an adult—a conception of the good life. We can come to recognize our own neurotic behavior as inconsistent with our idealized self-concept as a rational, autonomous, and responsible adult. We can say that a drug addict has an interest in giving up a heroin habit even though he does not recognize that he has such an interest, because we know that his conception of the good life embraces health and the preservation of life and that the use of heroin is alien to that conception (Geuss, 1981).

Interests can also become distorted by extreme deprivation, and one can get stuck fulfilling physical or safety needs at the expense of the need for self-actualization. Interests become distorted by physical coercion, by self-deception, and by dependence-producing belief systems or ideologies that define our reality. The oppressed internalize the values of their oppressors. In the slave economy of an earlier period, slaves seldom questioned the assumptions of their slavery. Few women questioned the social expectations of stereotypic sex roles prior to the women's movement. Through conscientization, Freire (1970) helps learners to become aware not only of their needs but of the reasons for their needs.

To participate as a self-directed learner in the process of dialogue requires full knowledge about alternatives as well as freedom from self-deception and coercion. This freedom requires an understanding of the historical, cultural, and biographical reasons for one's needs, wants, and interests, especially when they are derived from ideological or neurotic distortions. Such self-knowledge is a prerequisite for autonomy in self-directed learning.

One's real interests—interests guided by an authentic meaning perspective—are the interests that one would prefer to have if the circumstances under which one lived were more advantageous, in the sense of involving more knowledge and greater freedom, than the circumstances that now prevail. If a woman who has always accepted the traditional stereotypic woman's role begins to feel that her present interests may be less consistent with her concept of the adult life that she wants to live than the interests of her more emancipated friends are, their interests are her real interests. She would know what she wanted if she could know what she could want. Real interests are the interests we would form if we had more perfect knowledge and freedom, if we were better able to participate in ideal discourse. One of the most significant tasks of continuing education is to precipitate and facilitate this kind of learning for perspective transformation.

Uncritically assimilated meaning perspectives can reflect such distorting ideological assumptions as sexual or racial stereotypes. They can be distorted by erroneous assumptions about the nature and use of knowledge, such as assumptions involving reification or arbitrary conversion of a description into a prescription, as is often done with life stages. Meaning perspectives can also be distorted by failure to understand the function that the perspective fulfills, as when it impedes full participation in dialogue by supporting domination and repression or when it masks social injustice. Another source of distortion is errors in understanding one's true motives for accepting a given meaning perspective. As self-directed learners, we can learn to examine critically and to understand the reasons for the psychocultural assumptions that impede our ability to acquire meaning through unfettered participation in dialogue.

The obvious lesson here is that self-directed learners can operate at several different levels of rationality, morality, and sophistication. Distorted meaning perspectives generate distorted learning needs. In a limited sense, learners can be self-directed even though they suffer from acute tunnel vision. Their self-directed learning efforts may be motivated by venality, bigotry, viciousness, self-deception, and even self-destructiveness. They can assess their needs, set objectives, plan their learning experiences, carry them out, and evaluate them. To what learning needs or interests should an adult educator attend? Clearly, he or she should attend to the ones that help learners to move in the direction of more authentic meaning perspectives and that enable them to participate fully and freely in dialogue so that they can come to understand their experience better while preserving the rights of others to do the same.

Continental theorists Jurgen Habermas and Michel Foucault have helped us to understand that participants in a dialogue have a special obligation both to assess critically the initial premises of the propositions being argued and to recognize that knowledge is contingent on ideologies involving authority and power. These dependence-producing ideologies can be economic, religious, political, occupational, bureaucratic, psychological, educational, or technological. Critically reflective learning can reveal how traditional social practices and institutional arrangements contrive to legitimize and support ideologies that are inimical both to a more authentic meaning perspective and to the idea of free and open dialogue. Through perspective transformation, a self-directed learner can often see the necessity of taking collective action to make institutions more responsive to the learning needs of those whom they serve.

This is the reason why continuing educators find education for social action an integral part of their mission. We have the obligation to help learners to understand the alternatives and practical consequences of such action. Our function is not to lead or organize for collective action but to help learners become aware of the cultural contradictions that oppress them, research their own problems, build confidence, examine action alternatives, anticipate consequences, identify resources, educate others to the problem, foster participation and leadership, and assess relevant experience.

Not every educator in every situation can assume responsibility for facilitating the learning involved in taking collective action. Some will be able to work directly at this kind of education. Those who provide the public with diversified educational programs can commit resources to make such education available. The rest of us can fulfill our obligations by helping learners become aware of how cultural forces have structured their concepts of themselves, their roles, and their relationships. We can provide them with alternative perspectives for understanding how social practices and institutions can be modified so as to create a society in which adults can be enfranchised to participate fully as self-directed learners in the quest for the meaning of their lives.

It is precisely this enfranchisement that provides the common denominator uniting continuing educators with such apparently diverse goals as intellectual development, cognitive development, self-actualization, democratic participation, emancipation, and social action. All these dimensions of human development are essential to assure the fullest participation in dialogue as self-directed learners. And, this means full enfranchisement — a human entitlement — to explore fully the meaning of our experience and to realize the value potential in nature.

References

Bateson, G. *Steps to an Ecology of Mind*. New York: Basic Books, 1972.

Freire, P. *Pedagogy of the Oppressed*. New York: Herder and Herder, 1970.

Gagne, R. M. *The Conditions of Learning*. (Rev. ed.) New York: Holt, Rinehart and Winston, 1972.

Geuss, R. *The Idea of a Critical Theory: Habermas and the Frankfurt School*. Cambridge, England: Cambridge University Press, 1981.

Habermas, J. *Knowledge and Human Interests*. (J. J. Shapiro, Trans.) Boston: Beacon Press, 1971.

Hanson, N. R. "Reduction: Scientists Are Not Confined to the H-D Method." In L. Krimerman (Ed.), *Nature and Scope of Social Science*. New York: Appleton-Century-Crofts, 1981.

Knowles, M. *Self-Directed Learning: A Guide for Learners and Teachers*. New York: Cambridge Book, 1975.

Lakoff, G., and Johnson, M. *Metaphors We Live By.* Chicago: University of Chicago Press, 1980.

McCarthy, T. *The Critical Theory of Jurgen Habermas.* Cambridge, Mass.: M.I.T. Press, 1979.

Mezirow, J. *Education for Perspective Transformation: Women's Reentry Programs in Community Colleges.* New York: Center for Adult Education, Teachers College, 1975.

Mezirow, J. "Perspective Transformation." *Adult Education,* 1978, *28* (2), 100–110.

Mezirow, J. "A Critical Theory of Adult Learning and Education." *Adult Education,* 1981, *32* (1), 3–23.

Nottingham Andragogy Group. *Towards a Developmental Theory of Andragogy.* Adults: Psychological and Educational Perspectives series. Nottingham: University of Nottingham, 1983.

Powell, J. W. *Learning Comes of Age.* New York: Association Press, 1956.

Schon, D. "Generative Metaphor: A Perspective on Problem Setting in Social Policy." In A. Ortony (Ed.), *Metaphor and Thought.* Cambridge, England: Cambridge University Press, 1979.

Jack Mezirow is professor of adult and continuing education and director, Center for Adult Education, at Teachers College, Columbia University, New York City.

Successful implementation of self-directed learning opportunities depends largely on how well researchers and practitioners are able to bridge the gap between theory and practice.

Bridging the Theory–Practice Gap in Self-Directed Learning

Ralph G. Brockett
Roger Hiemstra

There is considerable research and theory into self-directed learning, as Brookfield and Mezirow note in Chapters One and Two. The purpose of this chapter is to build a bridge between their discussion of theory and research and the remaining chapters, which focus on particular areas in which self-directed learning can or does operate.

As Figure 1 shows, we see this chapter as a filtering device that distills theory and research into several areas. This chapter focuses on four issues: the learner's readiness for self-direction in learning, the teaching and learning process advocated for work with self-directed learners, policy considerations related to self-directed learning, and ethical issues relative to the implementation of self-directed learning concepts.

Self-Directedness: An All-or-Nothing Concept?

A clear understanding of how key concepts are defined is essential when we attempt to translate theory into practice. Such is the case with self-directed learning. While a detailed review of the ways in which various authors have conceptualized self-directedness is beyond the scope of this discussion, it is crucial to theory and practice to know whether self-directedness is

S. Brookfield (Ed.). *Self-Directed Learning: From Theory to Practice.* New Directions for Continuing Education, no. 25. San Francisco: Jossey-Bass, March 1985.

Figure 1. A Depiction of the Filtering Feature of Chapter Three

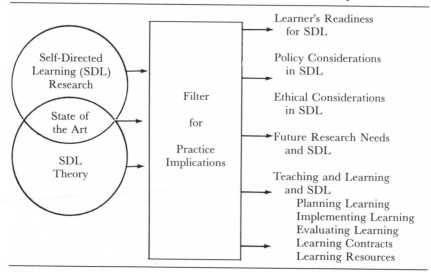

an all-or-nothing phenomenon or whether it varies with particular individuals and learning situations. In other words, is self-directedness best viewed as a dichotomous concept or as a continuous concept?

In a thought-provoking discussion of cognitive style, Even (1982) has suggested that persons who exhibit a field-independent learning style are likely to benefit from a self-directed emphasis but that field-dependent learners, who tend to have more of a social orientation, are not as likely to succeed in self-directed learning efforts. She illustrates this point by stating that the field-independent learners—those who tend toward self-directedness—prefer the lecture technique over interactive approaches, such as discussion and small-group tasks. Further, those persons are likely to prefer a teacher who is formal and highly structured over a teacher who is warm and supportive. Insomuch as this viewpoint does not address the potential interactive nature of psycho-social variables relative to self-directedness, one could argue that the field independence–field dependence model, as presented by Even, views self-directedness as a quality that is present in some individuals but not in others and thus that the model seems to embody a dichotomous view of self-directedness.

In their recent model of lifelong learning, Mocker and Spear (1982) draw a distinction between formal, nonformal, informal, and self-directed learning modes. These categories are represented in their model by two-by-two matrix based on who controls the objectives and the means for a learning situation—the institution or the learner. While Mocker and Spear view their model as a matrix, one can see the idea of a continuum in the model. For instance, formal learning refers to situations where the institution retains control over the objectives and means. In contrast, self-directed learning implies learner control of both elements. Both nonformal and informal learning involve some control both by learners and by institutions: Thus, they both lie at some point between the two extremes of the continuum.

Is self-directedness best viewed as a dichotomy or as a continuum? As Brookfield states in Chapter One, true self-directed learning can rarely if ever be achieved in institutional settings. By their very nature, institutions impose limits on self-direction. As a case in point, take the higher education setting. While an individual instructor may be deeply committed to the value of promoting self-direction in the classroom, the realities of grades and formally scheduled class meetings place a degree of structure on the learning situation that precludes total self-direction. Bauer addresses this dilemma in Chapter Four.

The attempt to understand self-directed learning as a continuum poses another problem. The continuum view implies that the degree of self-directedness varies considerably from individual to individual. Indeed, research involving the Self-Directed Learning Readiness Scale (SDLRS) has accentuated the differences that exist among individuals in skills and attitudes related to self-directedness.

When we attempt to promote self-direction in learning, we must bear two points in mind. First, since individuals vary in their readiness for self-direction, it is important for facilitators of adult learning to understand that they may have to assist some learners to become more self-directed. Second, it is important to avoid the pitfall of viewing self-directed learning as the best way to learn. With the great diversity that exists both in learning styles and in reasons for learning, it is extremely shortsighted to advance such an argument. Perhaps it is more appropriate to think of self-directed learning as an ideal mode of learning for certain individuals and for certain situations.

Facilitating Self-Directed Learning

Identifying the implications of these ideas for teaching is predicated on the notion that nearly all humans are capable of a degree of self-direction in their choices of learning approach, learning resources, and validation or evaluation techniques. This notion is akin to the critical theory assumptions described by Mezirow in Chapter Two. Unfortunately, much of the teaching used with adult learners, especially by individuals who have not had training in the teaching of adults, appears to be based on principles more of teacher-directed learning than of self-directed learning. Thus, we contend that considerable human potential is thwarted because learners are not able to take increased responsibility for learning that will be meaningful for them.

Teaching Strategy for Self-Directed Learners. Many continuing education authorities support the use of a variety of teaching and learning resources, facilitator teaching roles, and an active role by adult students during the entire teaching and learning process. In Chapter One, Brookfield refers to the findings of much research on self-directed learning over the past decade that many adult learners express a preference for self as a resource in and director of learning.

Such a role often includes participation in activities as diverse as assessing personal needs, planning learning activities, acquiring or developing certain learning resources, sequencing learning activities, and assuming responsibility for personal progress. However, for these activities to take place in such a way that such issues as quality, motivation, and institutional support can be addressed, especially for learning situations where some connection with an institution is necessary, desired, or expected, a learning partnership between the learner and an instructor is necessary.

As an example of what can happen when this learning partnership is applied to practice, a nontraditional graduate program at Syracuse University was set up with a major emphasis on the learner–instructor alliance. In September 1982, a Weekend Scholar program was established. The program enabled a student to earn a master's degree in adult education entirely through weekend courses. One of the assumptions underlying the development of this program was that successful participants would have the ability to assume a high degree of self-direction in meeting program expectations while maintaining professional and personal responsibilities that prevented them from participating in a late afternoon or early evening schedule of courses. All four faculty members who work with this program, which is currently operating at three locations in upstate New York, use a teaching and learning process whereby learners and instructors negotiate a learning contract establishing each individual's goals, strategies, and evaluation criteria for the particular subject matter under study. Both formative and summative evaluation efforts have shown that the combination of contracting with the faculty's commitment to learning partnerships has resulted in successful accomplishment of course and degree requirements. In addition, learners exhibit more positive attitudes about learning, the instructional process, and the program than had been anticipated. (The AEGIS program discussed in Chapter Four is a similar initiative at the doctoral level.)

The Role of the Instructor. What is the role of the instructor? An answer to this question must begin with the suggestion that traditional expectations tied to beliefs involving the dispensation of knowledge by experts to eager learners are incompatible with the model of personal ownership advocated in this chapter. This is not to suggest that such techniques as lecturing, Socratic dialogue, and standardized testing cannot be used in an interactive teaching and learning process. As a matter of fact, many learners deliberately choose to include such techniques or procedures in their personal learning plan. However, we wish to suggest that it is crucial for the successful teacher in self-directed learning situations to use facilitation techniques and to serve primarily as a manager of the teaching–learning transaction, not as an information provider. This implies that a facilitator must be able to tap a wide range of interpersonal helping skills, such as empathy, respect, and genuineness (Brockett, 1983).

The role of the manager differs from what often appears to be the norm in traditional teaching–learning situations — an authoritarian role whereby the teacher, in either an autocratic or a benevolent manner, adopts an expert posture and expects learners to recall and recite everything that they have been told or that they have read in the books assigned. Thus, the notions of interactiveness and potentiality, which encourage and indeed expect learners to take responsibility for their own learning, are of particular importance. Significant by-products for learners are positive feelings toward the subject matter, desire to explore the area of knowledge further, follow-up learning activities, and positive attitudes toward the total learning experience. Programs, such as Weekend Scholar and AEGIS, that attempt to make a high level of self-direction a vital part of the process are likely to be successful to the extent that facilitators are willing to shed the role of transmitter of content.

Tools for Self-Directed Learning. Just as a move toward increased self-directedness implies a changed role for the instructor, so can a number of tools be used to facilitate the learning process. Learning contracts and written materials designed for proactive use are two such tools.

Learning contracts have come into increasingly widespread use in recent years, especially in nontraditional higher education settings. Essentially, a learning contract is a written plan in which an individual documents, in varying degrees of detail, what and how he or she intends to learn in a given learning experience. The learning contract serves as a tool for communication between the learner and the facilitator. A major difficulty faced by most facilitators who advocate a self-directed approach is keeping track of the wide range of learning activities in which students choose to engage. The contract provides a written record of each student's proposed learning activities. In this way, it serves as a quality control mechanism. In addition, the contract offers learners a guide for planning the learning experience. While learning contracts can play a valuable role in enhancing the self-directed learning process, it is important to remember that the contract is only a tool — a means to an end.

Written learning materials are frequently identified as an important resource for continuing education. However, most discussions of materials have tended to focus on materials for programmed instruction or for adult basic education or high school equivalency programs. The use of written materials as resources for proactive learning in a self-directed mode has received little attention. However, such an approach could have important implications for adult learning opportunities in such areas as nontraditional higher education, continuing professional education, and programming in rural and isolated settings. Brockett (1984) has developed a model that asks a number of questions important to the process of planning and developing written materials for proactive learning.

Facilitating Self-Directed Learning. A number of instructional roles are related to work with self-directed learners. Facilitators can serve as one of many possible content resources. They can locate resources and present new information pertaining to derived learner needs. They can arrange for, manage, and employ a variety of resources necessary to accomplish learning goals. They can use a wide variety of learning techniques and supportive instructional devices to maintain learner interest and to present certain types of information. They can stimulate the interest and motivation of learners toward the chosen content areas. They can help learners to develop positive attitudes and feelings of independence relative to learning. They can promote discussion, questioning, and self-directed inquiry skills, and they can serve both to evaluate learner progress and to stimulate self-evaluation by learners. All these issues are addressed in Smith (1983).

Policy Recommendations for Self-Directed Learning

The development of educational policy is a difficult and often a complicated activity. It requires a multidisciplinary view, recognition of the complex nature of most problems, and the bringing together of a great deal of information, opinion, and existing practice. Implementation of such policy usually requires considerable care, dedication, and patience. The word *policy* can refer to rules, procedures, directives, and even traditions. In essence, a policy is a course of action recommended for accomplishing an organizational goal.

As a way of exploring the relation of policy development to self-directed learning, Hiemstra (1980) conducted a workshop that led to the development of a set of policies that aids organizations as they consider the implementation of self-directed learning concepts. The policies were conceptualized for three groups: adult learners, continuing educators, and continuing education agencies. During the workshop, a variety of implementation suggestions were derived for each of the policy recommendations offered here.

Adult Learners. The workshop developed eleven recommendations for adult learners: (1) The first step in recognizing our unlimited learning potential is to recognize that each of us is a worthwhile learner. (2) To gain self-acceptance, to capitalize on our assets, and to set personal goals, we must examine our strengths and weaknesses objectively. (3) To ensure continuous growth in our learning efforts, we must develop and strengthen our own internal mechanisms for reinforcement. (4) We must understand our own cognitive styles in order to shape our learning experiences for that style. (5) In order to enhance our efficiency and effectiveness, we must seek objective, individualized assistance in the planning and processing of learning projects. (6) To obtain direction, resources, and support, we must join and participate in learner advocate groups. (7) To capitalize on synergistic learning efforts, we must form autonomous learning groups. (8) To enhance our self-esteem and validate our progress, we need reinforcement and encouragement from others. (9) To ensure that we control our own learning, we must give ourselves the same status and respect that we accord to our teachers. (10) To ensure relevant and meaningful learning experiences, we must actively seek and take responsibility for our education. (11) To actualize our own learning potential, we must govern our time, space, and energy for learning projects.

Continuing Educators. The workshop developed three recommendations for continuing educators: (1) Research in continuing education must explore components of self-directed learning that have not already been studied. (2) In conjunction with their respective institutions, continuing educators must use the theories and practices of self-directed learning in classroom content and application efforts. (3) Continuing educators must help the agencies serving adults to incorporate the concepts of self-directed learning into their standard operating procedures.

Continuing Education Agencies. The workshop developed five recommendations for continuing education agencies: (1) Agencies, organizations, and institutions must provide administration, faculty, and staff with opportunities to become knowledgeable about published research on self-directed adult learning. (2) Agencies, organizations, and institutions must develop and maintain measures or criteria for accountability and evaluation. (3) Agencies, organizations, and institutions must provide support services that help self-directed adult learners to adjust to educational activities and any related changes. (4) Agencies, organizations, and institutions must conduct research on participation trends and interests. (5) Agencies, organizations, and institutions must provide environments that accommodate and facilitate self-directed learning.

It is obvious that the preceding policy recommendations represent only a few of those that are both possible and needed. For example, policies can be determined for a variety of levels or contexts other than those just described, including government, professional associations, and many specific programs and agencies. One appropriate point of departure for the policy development process is consideration of some ethical issues concerning self-directed learning that may require us to question even the appropriateness of policy development.

Ethical Questions in Self-Directed Learning

The idea of self-directed learning is not new. History abounds with examples of individuals—ranging from Socrates and Alexander the Great to Benjamin Franklin and Harry Truman—who have successfully taken charge of their own learning. Yet, only in recent years have continuing educators embraced the concept and begun to identify strategies for assisting adults to become more effective self-directed learners. As the emphasis on working with self-directed learners increases, it is vital for educators who wish to bridge the gap between theory and practice to examine a number of questions about the ethical implications of intervention with self-directed learners.

Singarella and Sork (1983) have noted that continuing education practitioners lack a literature on ethics. In the view of Singarella and Sork, questions related to the basic mission of continuing education and to the educator's allegiances to individuals, institutions, and society pose key ethical issues that continuing educators need to explore.

Explorations of the ethical questions related to self-directed learning need to address two dimensions: the relationship between learner and facilitator, and institutional issues. With regard to the first—the relationship between learner and facilitator—at least two questions surface immediately. First, can facilitator intervention be detrimental to the learning process in some situations? Facilitators often assume that they can help individuals to become more efficient self-directed learners. Indeed, for many learners, as research (Tough, 1979) points out, efficiency is a primary reason for preferring the self-planned approach to learning. This is particularly true when learning is instrumental to some other outcome, such as career advancement. However, we also know that many adults engage in learning for the sake of learning itself. In such expressive learning endeavors, the means are at least as important as the ends.

As an example, consider two individuals who wish to study local history. One learner has limited time for study and a schedule that does not permit regular attendance at class sessions. For this person, convenience and efficiency are the essential considerations. The other individual, who does not have the same time constraints, uses interest in local history as a springboard for visits to historical sites and museums in the area, where she meets and talks with other local history enthusiasts. It is appropriate to consider both individuals as self-directed learners. Yet, their needs as learners are very different. The facilitator who works with self-directed learners has a responsibility to understand and respect the individual learner's real needs. Such understanding can be achieved to a large extent by recognizing that, for some individuals, the learning process is at least as important as the outcome.

The second ethical consideration in the learner–facilitator relationship pertains to the issue of quality. Critics of nontraditional continuing education often argue that such opportunities are "watered down" or "quick and dirty" ways of pursuing learning. Others argue that, since self-directed learning implies a high degree of learner control, the facilitator has a convenient excuse for not preparing. In reality, the facilitation of self-directed learning is a very demanding responsibility. As pointed out earlier, the facilitator of self-directed learning opportunities needs to adopt a number of roles and skills that are very different from those of the traditional content-centered teacher. Herein lies the ethical issue. While some educators may misunderstand the meaning and process of self-directed learning and while a few may see the approach as a way of jumping on the latest bandwagon, the facilitator who truly understands and respects the self-directed learning process will strive to refocus, but certainly not to diminish, the nature of his or her responsibility to the learner.

The ethical issues just addressed—namely, the appropriateness of intervention and the provision of high-quality learning experiences—can also be addressed on an institutional level. For instance, institutions eager to identify potential new audiences may view self-directed learning as a way of serving persons whom they have not been able to reach in the past. When such efforts are undertaken with a clear sense of purpose and a commitment to the ideals of self-directed learning, they can be viewed as a response to an identified need. However, there is potential for abuse when the attractive prospect of self-directed learning is used to entice people into one type of program, and their needs might better be met by another approach, perhaps one that lies outside the realm of the institution.

The attitude of the institution is crucial for questions of quality. Institutions engaged in programs designed for self-directed learners need to consider such questions as these: Is this a learning experience that learners can better achieve on their own outside an institutional setting or in another type of institution? Will this program serve learners who would otherwise not be reached? Given the resources and policies of the institution, is it possible to meet the needs of self-directed learners with high-quality programming? Is the institution willing to commit to the trade-offs—decreased control and flexible program requirements—that are necessary to serve self-directed learners?

These questions do not exhaust the possibilities. Rather, they serve to indicate some issues that institutional programming for self-directed learners needs to consider. The question of ethics is crucial when we consider the future of research, theory, and practice in self-directed adult learning. Continuing educators would be well advised to consider these issues in greater depth in the future.

Conclusion

To serve as a bridge between the chapters on theory and research that precede and the situation-specific, illustrative chapters that follow, this chapter has sought to identify some issues that are vital to the implementation of self-directed learning. Such considerations as individual differences in self-directedness, facilitator roles and strategies, policy development, and ethical issues are important in attempts to implement self-directed learning in a wide range of settings, such as cultural institutions and institutions of higher education, as well as with diverse populations, such as older adults and health professionals.

While the ultimate value of self-directed learning lies in its implementation by individual learners, a strong theory and research base can make an invaluable contribution to informed practice. Continuing educators need to make frequent trips across the bridge that separates theory and practice.

40

References

Brockett, R. G. "Facilitator Roles and Skills." *Lifelong Learning: The Adult Years,* 1983, *6* (5), 7–9.

Brockett, R. G. "Developing Written Learning Materials: A Proactive Approach." *Lifelong Learning: An Omnibus of Practice and Research,* 1984, *7* (5), 16–18, 28.

Even, M. J. "Adapting Cognitive Style Theory in Practice." *Lifelong Learning: The Adult Years,* 1982, *5* (5), 14–16, 27.

Hiemstra, R. *Policy Recommendations Related to Self-Directed Learning.* Occasional Paper No. 1. Syracuse, N.Y.: Administrative and Adult Studies, Syracuse University, 1980.

Mocker, D. W., and Spear, G. E. *Lifelong Learning: Formal, Nonformal, Informal, and Self-Directed.* Columbus, Ohio: ERIC Clearinghouse on Adult, Career, and Vocational Education, 1982.

Singarella, T. A., and Sork, T. J. "Questions of Values and Conflict: Ethical Issues for Adult Education." *Adult Education Quarterly,* 1983, *33* (4), 244–251.

Smith, R. M. (Ed.). *Helping Adults Learn How to Learn.* New Directions for Continuing Education, no. 19. San Francisco: Jossey-Bass, 1983.

Tough, A. M. *The Adult's Learning Projects: A Fresh Approach to Theory and Practice in Adult Learning.* Austin, Texas: Learning Concepts, 1979.

Ralph G. Brockett is assistant professor of adult and higher education at Montana State University, Bozeman. When he was on the adult education faculty at Syracuse University, he helped to develop the Weekend Scholar program, and he cochaired the Task Force on Self-Directed Learning of the Commission of Professors of Adult Education.

Roger Hiemstra is professor and chair of the Adult Education Program at Syracuse University, Syracuse, New York. A past president of the Commission of Professors of Adult Education, he has been actively involved with the editorial boards of several publications in the field of adult education, and his research and writing on self-directed adult learning have spanned more than a decade.

*Can self-directed learning principles form the core of a total
doctoral program in adult and continuing education within
a traditional graduate school?*

Self-Directed Learning
in a Graduate Adult
Education Program

Barbara A. Bauer

The Adult Education Guided Independent Study (AEGIS) program is an
experimental alternative to the traditional doctoral program in the adult and
continuing education specialization in the Department of Higher and Adult
Education at Teachers College, Columbia University. In existence since 1981,
it provides an option to the fifty-year-old traditional program, which was the
first doctoral program of its kind. The AEGIS program was conceived of by
Jack Mezirow, professor of adult and continuing education and coordinator of
that field of study at Teachers College, in an attempt to adapt the principles of
adult education theory to the practice of doctoral education.

Participants

The AEGIS program is designed for a particular student clientele:
senior professionals with substantial experience in program development,
administration of continuing education, staff development, or training who
wish to earn a doctorate in two or three years. They are able to undertake this
study without having to relinquish their full-time employment or change locations in order to attend Teachers College. Participants come from three major

S. Brookfield (Ed.). *Self-Directed Learning: From Theory to Practice.* New Directions
for Continuing Education, no. 25. San Francisco: Jossey-Bass, March 1985.

areas of practice: higher education, business and industry, and health education. A variety of other institutional and community service settings is also represented.

The AEGIS program is now in its third year of operation with twenty-four male and forty-four female registrants. The first group was admitted in fall 1981, two groups entered in fall 1982, another group entered in fall 1983, and a new group was selected for fall 1984. The first dissertation defense was held in December 1983, and, of the remaining active participants who began the program in 1981, half graduated with the Ed.D. degree in May 1984.

The requirements that applicants must meet in order to be considered for the program are more stringent than the requirements for persons who apply to the traditional campus program. Applicants must have at least five years of full-time salaried titled professional employment in program development or administration of continuing education (the regular program requires two years). They must bring forty-five transferable graduate credits from a superior graduate record. They must provide an academic or professional writing sample indicating their ability to do doctoral-level work. They must offer proof that they have access to an academic or professional library in their community. They must explain why they need the AEGIS option, and they must demonstrate commitment to the practice of continuing education.

Careful screening of all application materials is followed by an on-campus interview for those who meet all entrance requirements. The interviews are conducted by a two-member faculty team. The final decisions are based on the screening and interview results. Each group is limited to between twenty and twenty-four participants.

Mission

The primary mission of the AEGIS program is to assist continuing education practitioners to exercise and further develop their own self-directedness. To this end, the program emphasizes five objectives: helping participants to acquire andragogical perspectives on their own learning processes and on the learning processes of the adults whom they serve; progressively transferring the responsibility for designing, conducting, and evaluating their own learning programs to participants; facilitating the growth of participants' critical analytical abilities in examining both their assumptions about themselves as educators and their practice of continuing education; assisting them to become aware of the theoretical contexts of problems in the field; and promoting their interest and skills in disciplined inquiry. These objectives are supported by the design of the curriculum and by the teaching and learning methods employed.

Special Program Features

Participants are brought in for a two-day orientation weekend in June in order to provide them with guidance in their summer readings and to get them started thinking critically about issues in the field of continuing education.

They are encouraged to begin networking among themselves and to form support groups. Each cohort progresses through two years of course work (six consecutive semesters, including summers) with the same group.

The course work begins in September with once-monthly all-day meetings. The day is divided into two three-hour seminars, with an hour at midday for lunch. The same schedule is followed in subsequent academic semesters. Between the monthly seminars, participants complete the course requirements on their own. Advisement is available by mail, telephone, and optional campus visits. During each of the two summers of course work, participants come on campus for a three-week intensive session and meet daily. They take core AEGIS courses as well as courses outside the department.

To promote participants' movement through the doctoral program, a special system of support services was set up within the department to function as liaison between the participants and various college offices. Participants are on campus only once a month during the academic year, and most come from outside the immediate New York City area. This means that the usual time-consuming activities required by the institution for regular students, such as registration, issuance of student identification, order and purchase of textbooks, filing for certification, and maintenance of doctoral status, must be managed through the AEGIS office. Such activities are handled by mail or in a few minutes while the participants are on campus. A fifteen-minute period is set aside before the first session of the monthly meeting for administrative business.

The Self-Directed Strategies Applied

While the process of writing a dissertation can be seen as a highly self-directed learning experience, the total doctoral program itself usually is not. Standards are set, and they must be met: There are credits to be documented, various courses are required, examinations have to be passed, and other institutional approvals must be gained along the way. Apart from electing some courses, students do not need to be exceptionally self-directed to complete their program of studies. However, the AEGIS program, which was set up as an option within a traditional graduate school of education, attempts to maximize opportunities for self-directed learning while charting alternate paths through the traditional institutional requirements.

The Curriculum: First Year. The fit of Knowles's (1975) basic understanding of self-directed learning with the AEGIS curriculum is evident. During the first semester, participants take the initiative, with the help of faculty, in diagnosing their learning needs. In a proseminar, they write a series of essays relating their prior professional experience to the concepts and issues of continuing education. They explore ideas in the literature that are new to them or that relate to areas of inquiry that interest them.

The AEGIS program views the learning contract as a primary vehicle for self-directed learning. Studies by Kasworm (1982), Caffarella (1983), and

Caffarella and Caffarella (1984) document the use and the effectiveness of learning contracts in formal graduate adult education. To ensure that participants are initiated early into the use of this instrument, they are asked to carry out a prototypical learning contract as part of the proseminar. Guidelines are provided to aid in developing the contracts. These guidelines include both the various components of learning contracts — general purpose, learning objectives, learning methods, criteria for assessment, evaluators, and work schedule — and specific recommendations for contract completion.

In a concurrent research methods seminar during the first semester, participants investigate qualitative methods and resources for disciplined inquiry into broad areas of interest in the field of continuing education. For their dissertations, they are encouraged to engage in qualitative research, unless they have had previous training in quantitative methods. In dissertation-planning seminars in the spring semester, the investigation begins to narrow down to particular areas of dissertation interest and to the particular methods and resources that individual participants might use to pursue their dissertation ideas. A draft proposal is the end product of this course.

During the same semester, participants meet in a readings seminar to consider the chief theoretical perspectives on adult learning and education and to develop their skills of critical analysis by scrutinizing the underlying value assumptions of these theories when put into practice. This process of critical reflectivity is seen as another vital dimension of self-directedness, moving practice out of the domain of unquestioningly accepted ideas and behavior into the realm of conscious evaluation and active choice.

An important feature of the program is that participants' work is evaluated on a pass-or-fail basis; no grades are given. Papers are returned as often as required with suggested revisions. When both participant and seminar leader are satisfied that the learner's goals have been met, the paper is considered complete, and a pass is awarded.

By the time participants enter the first summer session, they have been introduced to self-directed learning strategies, learning contracts, methods of qualitative research, and theories of adult learning and education, and they have begun formulating their own dissertation topics and methodologies.

Although their summer schedule includes an empirical methods research course and a preparation workshop for the certification examination (an essay-type examination given in January of the second year), the focal point of the daily three-week session is the contract-planning course. In this course, a learning contract is developed for each of three core courses scheduled for the following academic year: How Adults Learn, Program Development in Adult and Continuing Education, and Organization and Administration of Adult and Continuing Education.

Since the tie-in of the contract courses is germane to early dissertation planning, additional guidelines for contract formulation are provided at this time. These guidelines give participants two options in designing their learning contracts: They can use one or more of the three contracts to implement the dissertation, or they can use the contracts to explore areas not related to a dissertation topic. If the participant takes the first option, he or she can use the contracts in various ways to implement a dissertation: conducting a review of the literature or interpreting the work of one or more writers; using the contract to define a dissertation problem or alternative problems; drafting the chapter on methodology; developing one or more instruments (an interview schedule, program data inventory, questionnaire, scale, or set of critical incidents) and field testing the instruments; preparing a section for the dissertation dealing with the theoretical context of the problem and critically analyzing the assumptions, premises, and presuppositions; or undertaking fieldwork, administering the data-gathering instruments involved in carrying out the dissertation, or both.

Armed with a syllabus for each course and a draft proposal for a dissertation, small groups of seven or eight meet with faculty members for each of the core courses in daily work sessions. The purposes of these sessions are to enable participants to identify learning needs and goals relevant to the content of each course, to focus on resources, and to select strategies for the implementation of the learning that they plan. Participants help each other as well as themselves in tackling these important tasks. Participants are written into each other's contracts as evaluators when their areas of expertise and interest converge. This opportunity for extended, intensive contact among cohort members during the summer is seen as vital in solidifying smaller networks, which prove an invaluable source of professional, academic, and moral support to these adult learners negotiating such a fast-paced doctoral program.

The Curriculum: Second Year. During the fall semester of the second year, participants attend monthly half-day seminars in two of the contract courses: How Adults Learn and Program Development in Adult and Continuing Education. They read and discuss selected materials, write critically analytical papers on issues in the literature, and work to complete the two contracts drawn up the previous summer for these two courses. They also pursue ongoing dissertation advisement with their sponsors, usually firming up the dissertation proposal and passing an official acceptance hearing.

In January, participants take the certification examination. During the spring semester, they complete the contract for the Organization and Administration course, along with readings and discussion. Dissertation advisement continues. By the end of this semester, if a participant has chosen the option of using the learning contracts to implement the dissertation, three major parts of the dissertation can be well under way.

The last summer is dedicated to out-of-department grounding in two disciplines from which adult education draws heavily: social philosophy and adult development. The last workshop is designed by the participants, who focus on learning activities that they wish to pursue. When the second summer session ends, participants have completed the required coursework equivalent to forty-five graduate credits. Added to the forty-five transfer credits, the course work credits provide the ninety credits prescribed for the Ed.D. degree at Teachers College.

Participants continue individual advisement with their sponsors until they are ready to defend the dissertation. For most, the defense takes place during the seventh or eighth semester, that is, two and a half to three years after they enter the program.

Teaching and Advising. As facilitators of self-directed learning, the instructional staff have chosen not to rely on the traditional lecture mode of delivery. Formal presentations are limited to approximately twenty minutes for each three-hour session. The bulk of class time is dedicated to discussion of reading materials and to the sharing of professional expertise in the analysis of adult education literature and issues.

The largest share of the time is allocated to assignments with due dates, which include readings and issues papers. When assignments are received between sessions, professors read them and write extensive commentaries and suggestions for revisions. These are mailed back to the participants, and several telephone conversations initiated by the participants for advisement purposes usually ensue. While some participants live close enough to see professors on campus between the monthly sessions, most advisement is conducted by telephone during special hours set aside by the faculty for that purpose and at other times when participants so request.

Another important feature of planning stems from the acknowledgement that the ordinary custom of presenting students with a course syllabus during the first class of each semester is unsuited for the AEGIS program. Recognizing the participants' need for being able to plan well ahead for the organization of each semester's work, faculty provide course syllabi and assignments at least two months in advance of the beginning of the semester. Possession of these materials allows these full-time professional working adults to integrate course work demands and due dates into predictable work and personal schedules. With some lead time, they can get a head start on readings so that unpredicted crises that arise within the semester itself need not disrupt their course work progress.

The Problems Encountered

The AEGIS attempt to apply self-directed learning principles to a graduate program in adult education has encountered several problems. One set of problems has to do with the incoming participants' competencies for self-directed learning. Another set centers on the constraints posed by institutional and program requirements, while a third set of problems deals with the role of faculty. The perceptions discussed here have been reported in interviews conducted as part of a doctoral dissertation study (Bauer, 1985).

Levels of Self-Directedness. Although efforts are made at the time of screening and selection interviews to elicit evidence of self-directedness in individual applicants, no formal test is applied. Since all applicants are successful senior professionals in continuing educator roles, it is assumed that they possess many of the characteristics of self-directed persons. However, since most have been away from formal graduate education for some time, their ability to translate and transfer their self-directedness from the professional to the academic sphere is difficult to predict. Therefore, the range of need for structure differs greatly within a single group.

The varying levels of self-directedness become apparent to faculty during the first semester through performance on written assignments as well as through the nature and degree of direction necessary in advisement. Participants also quickly become aware of the range of competencies within the group. The discrepancies cause some frustration for them, but they are most often met with supportive concern and action in an effort to aid those who need the most guidance. Openness and willingness to change on the part of the less proficient individuals can sometimes allow them to learn to be more competent self-directed learners, but the demands of course work do not provide much time for catching up.

The problems that derive from the varying levels of self-directedness within the group can be addressed in two different ways. One is to develop more successful ways of predicting academic self-directedness for the time when applicants are being considered for admission. The other is to seek ways of strengthening these competencies in the participants who are most in need.

Institutional and Program Constraints. Because the program is part of the traditional departmental structure of Teachers College, it must maintain the same institutional standards for doctoral study. Participants must register at the beginning of each semester, their grades must be recorded at the end of each semester, they must take and pass the certification examination about midway through the program, they must take courses outside the department, they must meet difficult deadlines for written work, and they must conduct research worthy of an Ed.D. degree. These requirements necessarily place limitations on the degree of self-direction offered to participants.

The nature of the program itself precludes opportunities for self-direction available to students in the traditional campus program. Because the AEGIS program is structured so that course work is completed in two years, participants enter and move with their cohort through the two years of course work. They are registered as a group for the prescribed courses each semester, they have no choice in course selection, and they cannot lighten a particular semester's course load in order to accommodate unanticipated personal or work pressures.

Participants must be able to sacrifice such opportunities for self-direction in order to concentrate on and maximize the other more specific occasions where highly developed self-directing skills are needed. As mentioned earlier, these occasions center on the choice of content and methodology for the learning contracts and for the dissertation and on how the two shall blend. Participants are also presented with opportunities for critical questioning of the assumptions underlying their professional practice and for the restructuring of this base for future self-directed action in the company of close colleagues and fellow learners. Finally, self-direction is apparent in participants' management of their own time and resources in achieving their learning objectives.

The Role of Faculty. Faculty involvement in a program like the AEGIS program presents challenges not usually found in doctoral programs. In more traditional situations, there is an accepted mode of course construction and a well-established rhythm of weekly and seasonal patterns that flows with the stream of the whole institution. Within this context, it is easy for professors to allocate their time for pursuit of their research interests.

The AEGIS program represents a significant break with this mode. The program has an insistent and stepped-up rhythm of its own. Since all faculty members teach in both the AEGIS and the regular campus program, they have to organize two different semester schedules. AEGIS course syllabi and assignments must be prepared months in advance to give participants the opportunity to plan their own academic, professional, and personal schedules.

Pressure mounts when assignments are received. Instructors try to read them as soon as possible and provide participants with comments and suggestions for revisions or for proceeding with subsequent assignments. With participants under pressure to meet a series of due dates, immediate feedback is a necessity.

Managing the continuous one-to-one contact with participants presents another dimension. Because participants are most often pursuing their own work-related inquiries, advisement must be tailored to each individual's needs. While this challenge has the concomitant advantage of keeping the faculty in direct contact with what is going on in field situations, it can also stretch the range of resource expertise beyond a particular professorial specialization.

Such active involvement in participants' professional interests and needs limits the time that faculty have available for the pursuit of their own research interests. This can be especially threatening for an untenured professor, since research and publication are vital in re-appointment and tenure decisions. Whether faculty can sustain this type of commitment for an indefinite period of time has yet to be determined. Although there are clear positive factors—being able to practice continuing education theory in graduate education and to function in a team-like educational environment that extends the spirit of collaborative learning to faculty planning for the program—maintaining an overall balance between teaching and research activities is crucial.

Conclusion

This chapter has described one attempt to place self-directed learning at the center of a doctoral program in adult education. Five cohorts have been recruited in four years, and half the first cohort has graduated in the prescribed three-year period. The other groups of participants are on schedule with course work, and they will be able to complete their dissertations during their third year. A few participants have had to withdraw along the way, most because of pressures external to the program.

Learning contracts have proved effective learning tools within the given courses as well as effective building blocks for dissertations. Participants express satisfaction with the use of learning contracts and with the possibility for guided independent study, and many have been able to incorporate elements of both into their professional work.

Most faculty have been able to keep the demands made on their time by this teaching commitment in balance with the demands of their own research needs. The institution as a whole has been supportive of the program and has cooperated in working out alternative paths through the bureaucratic necessities.

The program has undergone considerable refinement since its inception, and in its present form it seems to be a viable option for graduate education. With careful and consistent monitoring, the program should be able to continue to provide a maximum amount of self-directedness within the rapid pace of a nontraditional option for the study of adult education at the doctoral level.

References

Bauer, B. A. "The Adult Education Guided Independent Study (AEGIS) Program: An Administrative Case Study." Unpublished doctoral dissertation, Teachers College, Columbia University, 1985.

Caffarella, R. S. "Fostering Self-Directed Learning in Postsecondary Education: The Use of Learning Contracts." *Lifelong Learning*, 1983, *7* (3), 7–19, 24–25.

Caffarella, R. S., and Caffarella, E. P. "Self-Directedness and Learning Contracts in Graduate Education." In *Lifelong Learning Research Conference Proceedings*, no. 4. College Park: Department of Agriculture and Extension Education, University of Maryland, 1982.

Kasworm, C. E. "An Exploratory Study of the Development of Self-Directed Learning as an Instructional/Curriculum Strategy." In *Lifelong Learning Research Conference Proceedings*, no. 6. College Park: Department of Agriculture and Extension Education, University of Maryland, 1984.

Knowles, M. S. *Self-Directed Learning: A Guide for Learners and Teachers*. New York: Cambridge Book, 1975.

Barbara A. Bauer is the program administrator of the AEGIS Program at Teachers College, Columbia University, New York City.

For inquiries of all kinds, libraries and museums invite useful
engagements with information and memorable encounters with objects.

Self-Directed Learning
in Cultural Institutions

David Carr

Cultural institutions have many forms in communities everywhere, and
everywhere they do similar things. Museums, libraries, historical societies,
zoos, aquariums, ancient sites, restored villages, botanical gardens, forest pre-
serves, wildlife refuges, famous homes, planetariums—all these assemble
information and objects for public inquiry and use. They require no examinations for entrance, they conduct no evaluations of individual users, and they
offer no credentials on exit. They are available to learners of all ages, and so
they can meet the needs of families. No one is required by law or convention
to use them, yet millions of learners do, freely and for diverse reasons: useful
learning, continuity with the past, pure pleasure.

Although the nature of the invitation offered by any environment can
be unclear, cultural institutions could well be called *invitational environments.*
Clearly, such places invite citizens to visit: They are listed in directories and
guidebooks, their offerings are advertised, and they attract attention to special
events. However, there are differences between visiting cultural institutions
and using them just as there are differences between visiting and using a fire
station or a bank.

In cultural institutions, distinctions between visit and use might reflect
the nature of the learning invitation offered. The museum or library that com-
municates directly to its community the idea of using its collections to meet an

S. Brookfield (Ed.). *Self-Directed Learning: From Theory to Practice.* New Directions
for Continuing Education, no. 25. San Francisco: Jossey-Bass, March 1985.

agenda for learning has taken a stride toward creating a population of museum learners. Distinctions between visit and use might also reflect the nature of the investment elicited from the individual learner. The planetarium that invites a learner to explore private night thoughts in the presence of astral constellations adds personal dimensions to public experiences. Memory, imagination, and reverie are among them.

While the public qualities of cultural institutions — openness and freedom from prescription, satisfying contents, the pleasing tendency not to interfere with users — make personal dimensions attractive to self-directed learners, there are few supportive messages about self-directed learning in these environments. Often, logical paths or patterns for independent learning are tacit. Stimulating, current bibliographies or other messages about pertinent new knowledge are difficult to come by. Methods for documenting new learning or a memorable encounter are not always evident. Worse, certain barriers to independent learning are often present. Some of these barriers are easy to document: Helpful mediation is not always assured, explanatory texts are often obscure or dense, connections and processes for learning are not clearly articulated. Other barriers are less visible, since they reside in the imaginations of learners and educators, but they are no less sources of tension for self-directed learners.

Museums and libraries are visible public institutions, often creating a community intellectual center by their simple presence. Yet, learning experiences in these places are private, often deeply introspective. The importance of this subtle private function can be obscured or reduced by an institution's public social and cultural agendas. It is also likely that highly visible innovations are easier to finance in a climate of competition for elusive capital. Unfortunately, appropriate assistance to adult learners is not only difficult to see, it is also costly to provide. Services for children or schools are less difficult to justify. Innovations for adult learning may be seen as less promising and as less likely to generate the large numbers needed to document an institution's impact.

Once the decision to assist adult independent learners is made, however, tensions can follow from certain difficult tasks. What kind of help can be given that is at once timely, useful, and personal yet neither manipulative nor intrusive? How fully should data be preconstructed for the learner? How can learners be helped to encounter objects and texts? The primary difficulty — and the clearest source of tension — lies in finding the most fluent institutional voice and the most appropriate community messages.

Speaking to mature learners requires both the imagination needed to create inviting possibilities and the vision to include these possibilities with the public commitments of the cultural institution. Theodore Low (1942, p. 21) wrote about the museum as an educative and therefore social instrument that it "must be active, not passive, and it must always be intimately connected with the life of the people." The museum, Low wrote, must concentrate on the unmet needs of the adult public. One of Low's precursors was the neglected community genius John Cotton Dana, who led the Newark Public Library and who founded the Newark Museum seventy-five years ago. Unlike the "mausoleums of curios" that he derided, Dana's cultural institutions were designed to speak seriously to the adult citizens of Newark about what they were: skilled workers, aspiring community members, curious learners. Dana wrote (Lipton, 1979, pp. 24–25) that "a good museum attracts, entertains, arouses curiosity, leads to questionings—and thus promotes learning.... To use simple things to promote an intelligent and particular interest, a museum must apply to them the best skill it can acquire, infinite tact, and a constant sympathy." It is worth noting that a flourishing adult program continues at the Newark Museum today.

My intentions in this chapter are to describe issues and conditions of self-directed learning in cultural institutions and to advocate the integration of cultural institutions with other parts of the adult's configurations of education. Much of this chapter is written with museums in mind, but my hope is to offer a generic view that is relevant to all cultural institutions, whatever their content or purpose. At the center of these intentions is the assumption that the public purposes and values of cultural institutions converge with the private intentions of self-directed learners. There are few inquiries that cannot find in these places the insight that leads to personal knowledge.

Cultural Institutions as Invitational Environments

To think of cultural institutions as invitational environments is to suggest that there is an institutional voice which says, "Come in. This is an interesting place for free learning. What you encounter here can make a difference in your life." Though such invitations are rarely overt, they exist in the unspoken messages that surround libraries and museums and what they hold.

Ways of Knowing. The most obvious invitations to cultural institutions come from objects or contents themselves: rare artifacts, useful documents, historic objects, unusual specimens. But, it is not the intrigue of objects alone that attracts the self-directed learner to the museum or library rather than to the school. However strong the congruities between schools and cultural institutions may be, they offer fundamentally different conditions for knowing and thinking.

Both schools and cultural institutions are educative environments where an array of messages is displayed, and these messages make use of symbols and conventions that require literacy for full participation. Both schools and cultural institutions are concerned with the past and the future; they share an interest in preserving values, traditions, and systems. Human beings are present in each kind of environment, and the complex communities outside present demographic, intellectual, and avocational interests that the environment tends to reflect. In contrast, schools depend on teachers, treat learners in classes by age, follow prescriptive schedules and curricula, evaluate skills, offer credentials, require attendance by law, emphasize closed spaces, and attend less to objects and experiences than to talk and textbooks.

Museums and libraries foster autonomous individual learning, emphasize timelessness and breadth, and accept diverse learners, but they offer neither evaluations nor credentials, they do not require attendance by law or other authority, and they emphasize objects and experiences in the world outside. Cultural institutions are lifelong environments; their contents and messages attend to human beings across the life span. They are open to all, they are often free, and typically they are supported by public funds. These criteria help to define the educative characteristics of cultural institutions and to explain their appeal.

Every learner in the museum or library is invited to make choices, using texts and objects over time to answer questions and suggest new thinking. In these settings, learning occurs to the expansive, flexible, grasping mind that is able to envision and apply abstract concepts in life outside the environment. This challenges the imagination for several reasons. First, data in museums and libraries are rarely arranged in linear ways. Since there is often no clear direction, the learner must design his or her own useful, sensible path. Second, because these environments present broad images of sometimes distant worlds, learners must occasionally envision exotic contexts and vivify timeworn values. Third, in open and nondirective environments, learners must be clear and purposeful. To these challenges, add another: Because the learner is the source of design and inquiry and because the best path is not always clear, a strong tolerance for ambiguity is useful. So is a patient, responsive spirit.

The kinds of knowing available in cultural institutions may have been best described by Kenneth Boulding (1966), who argued that cultural institutions transmit developed images of the world. These images can involve logical or technical skills, scholarly knowledge, broad patterns, or other applicable insights about how the world works. In art museums, dreams, memories, or myths might be evoked. In museums of history or social science, the learner might weave strands of personal experience into the data at hand. In museums of natural history or of science and technology, the progress of living creatures toward a challenging future might be evoked. In all these, stories might be told. Libraries evoke different but no less powerful images or stories of passage and change. For self-directed learners in cultural institutions, such forms of order often represent intense investments of attention and articulation.

Constructions and Connections. Learning experiences in cultural institutions are examples of what Kelly (1963) calls *construing,* that is, of interpreting or framing an experience and so of giving it shape or meaning. For Kelly (p. 74), this framing is essential: "It is when man begins to see the orderliness in a sequence of events that he begins to experience them." Kelly writes elsewhere (1977, p. 4) that "to construe the surrounding world is to visualize it in more than one dimension." Learning is not a special or particular process, "not something that happens to a person on occasion; it is what makes him a person in the first place. . . . To construe is to hear the whisper of recurrent themes in the events that reverberate around us" (Kelly, 1963, p. 75).

Construction is a basic process of self-directed learning in cultural institutions, where information is generally available to learners without an implied path or design. Except in cases of preconstructed experiences, such as those in planetariums or guided tours, the learner experiences the environment without external direction. A plan or sequence may evolve as the environment and its experiences become clear and as the whisper of recurrent themes is heard. All passages in cultural institutions require the learner to reconstruct or repattern the data encountered in order to possess it usefully in relation to inquiries or interests at hand. Learning in cultural institutions means framing private meanings out of public encounters. In Jerome Bruner's (1973) memorable phrase, it means going beyond the information given.

Bruner has also said that "perceiving takes place in a tuned organism" (1973, p. 92), and Michael Polanyi (1958) has written powerfully about the knowledge that dwells within us. In the museum or library, the learner's inherent task is to match experiences of the moment with experiences embedded in memory and expectation. This matching process can be exhilarating. The learner is directly invested in such encounters with data, which essentially change one's relations with the world. These moments are continuous with the past, but at the same time they reveal and explain the importance of new and inviting unknowns. To learn in this way is not only to construe concepts and objects in new ways, it is to design a new image of the learning self in relation to future experiences.

Objects and Tools. In a culture as materialistic as ours, it is surprising to note that learners are rarely helped to learn from objects, to see them as messages about the world in which they emerged or to think of them as keys or tools for knowing. Providing such assistance is in the interest of cultural institutions, because it is the provision of tools, objects, and texts that moves a learner toward usefully organized information and memorable knowledge.

Objects and tools offer examples, applications, and contexts—historic, esthetic, personal—that enlarge the experiences of self-directed learners. When taken in detail, such objects and their connotations affect and enlarge emerging constructs. Consider a permanent and relatively accessible example, the full-scale diorama featuring American bison and pronghorn antelope displayed in the Hall of American Mammals in the American Museum of Natural History in New York City. Aside from the definitions of each species and the data offered in adjacent texts, the observer can notice geographic details of the landscape portrayed and the ecology of the region, including tacit interdependencies among the flora and fauna shown. Of the animals themselves, qualities of relative size, proportion, and external features are visible, as are more esthetic aspects, such as color, form, and texture. Biological relationships, such as symbiosis and mutualism, are demonstrable. Beyond these visible elements, there are stories to be told about the relation of the Native American to the bison, the effect of the westward migration on that relation, and the current status of the species in America.

Such inventories can be conducted for any number of other presentations in the same setting. By juxtaposing the resulting data, powerful constructs involving animal biology, ecology, and natural history can emerge. In other parts of the museum, the learner can see fossil precursors of the bison in North America, models of the bison hunt in Native American cultures, and documentation about the generic relationship between humans and nature. The bison-dependent Native American can usefully be compared with the caribou-dependent Eskimo. The museum shop offers texts about these topics, and the museum library is open to public use. In the library, such topics as *bison, American, ghost dance, the West,* and *Indians of North America* and such subheadings as *hunting, religion and mythology,* and *social life and customs* will yield pertinent information.

It is important to note that these learning tasks are not restricted by age, experience, or intellectual development; they will invite engaged learners at any level of expertise. Such inquiries require little more than energy, time, and broad, useful skills that we could describe as museum literacy. As in other new environments, these skills involve the decoding of signs and the reading of maps. But, they also involve the ability to learn from objects, to generalize across experiences, and to pursue an interlocking chain of data. These pursuit skills are rarely taught, even by the institutions in which they are most clearly applicable. They are not difficult to imagine, but they are challenging to sustain without assistance. Even when we are unassisted, however, our best questions offer lasting invitations. We might say that literacy in cultural institutions means fluent conversation in this language of questions.

Rather than a bison, the example just given could have centered instead on a local rodent or a prehistoric avian, a clay sculpture or a gold amulet, a collection of reed containers or of hunting implements—or any ancestor of man. The naive but useful questions used to organize our inquiry remain: What is here? What are its origins? How did it belong to its environment? What is its meaning over time? Do other things of this kind exist? How is it continuous with other objects or texts? What are its messages to my life? These echo the questions posed by the poet Paul Valery (1964) in his superb essay "Man and the Seashell": Who made this? Of what? And why?

The Invitation Offered. Cultural institutions offer an invitation to the adult self-directed learner that is at once personal and public. It is first an invitation to decide about the importance of an inquiry and its meaning to the learner. It is then an invitation to consider evidence in relation to the inquiry and its meaning. It is also an invitation to act in order to learn. This means several things: attending to objects and tools, observing and evaluating evidence, gathering pertinent documentation, experimenting with new combinations of data, crossing the boundaries of traditional disciplines, and organizing a coherent pattern of knowledge that is both useful and satisfying. Finally, the cultural institution offers an invitation to integrate its data and experiences with the continuities of one's life. These continuities — the interests, values, and information that shape and direct our instrumentality — are not accidental. Rather, they emerge as we make decisions and as we act appropriately to design learning.

Embedded in these invitational qualities are qualities of learning that fall under Bateson's (1972) obscure term *deutero-learning* or under Smith's (1982, 1983) more accessible formulation, *learning to learn.* In the cultural institution, self-directed learners become models for themselves. Learning to use the cultural institution in pursuit of one inquiry offers an enduring literacy or process that is useful in other, future tasks. The formative behaviors that constitute this learning involve asking good questions, seeking and using help, exploring ancillary networks of resources and persons, scanning the environment with attuned sensitivity, and recombining diverse experiences — work, travel, conversation — according to how they inform an evolving inquiry.

Conditions of Learning in Cultural Institutions

Although inquiries in cultural institutions can be defined by their conclusions — answers, data, products — they are more importantly defined by the intentions that begin them and by the information that flows through them.

Creating an Informed Inquiry. Questions must start somewhere, with something, although it may be little more than an obscure impulse to inquire. At those moments of beginning, the vague conditions of a satisfactory conclusion may be clearer than the conditions of a good question. But, the question is essential. Unlike learners in schools, self-directed learners in cultural institutions are responsible for the quality of both questions and answers. Useful ends follow only from the deliberate evolution of informed questions. A good question is often intensely subjective; it summarizes where a learner is in the bare landscape of a topic. It captures the immediate environment (what is known now) as well as the horizon (what is wanted). Good questions are rarely unitary. More often, they comprise a constellation or hierarchy of several logically connected questions, any one of which can be a useful point of entry. The language of a question matters very much: The success of any library search depends on precise descriptors, and the ambiguities that flavor an inquiry are captured best in the delicate shadings of words. A question and its language often carry tacit but diverting assumptions or powerful but unclear intuitions; these hidden dimensions can limit, direct, or otherwise alter the process of the inquiry. Certainly, a combination of knowns and unknowns informs every question.

Consequently, a good question begins with an open end, an answer that does not close the inquiry but that adjusts its focus or dimensions. A good question itself construes possible answers: It recognizes the boundaries of relevant evidence, it specifies fields and limits, and it suggests directions. Yet, it also transcends some boundaries: Good questions bear upon other questions. An inquiry may not only deliver a useful answer, it is also an informed passage to other problems or concepts. A carefully articulated question defines a perspective from which the self-directed learner can evaluate options, routines, and strategies for learning. This vantage can also include practical assessments of personal and institutional constraints.

Self-directed learners are likely to be engaged in complex lives outside the museum or library, and these external contexts are demanding, sometimes inflexible. Cultural institutions are themselves constraining, often formal, self-involved structures; they do not bend easily to meet the needs of self-directed learners for convivial access, order, process, and continuity. And last, they do not often assert a public agenda for learning—an essential need.

Useful Messages in Cultural Institutions. Because cultural institutions are public places for private learning, the tasks and processes of learners in them are frequently invisible, undocumented, and unassisted. Learners depend on messages from the institution itself about use. They need help to grasp the complex information given and to move beyond it by reconstructing it into useful patterns.

Cultural institutions might be described as conceptually dense: They offer rich images of a diverse world informed by abstract social, esthetic, and technical meanings. Often, these images are arranged according to specialized taxonomies and hierarchies. Consequently, the learner requires forms of public order that can be used to establish intellectual connections and technical continuities. Beyond the map, the guide, or the directional sign, the library or museum must make its paths and their permutations explicit.

Cultural institutions are inherently intellectual in that they demand a range of literacies for full participation. Learners must unlock or decode an intimidating number of information-laden objects, including texts, nonprinted media, artifacts, and computers. In this information-rich environment, the learner requires forms of public access to the literate behaviors demanded by the institution. Beyond readable directions and explanations, the library or museum must design orientations that foster independent use and that suggest useful forms of documentation. These messages are best delivered by human beings.

Cultural institutions are inherently experiential: As the act of construing implies, they require us to make selections, decisions, and engagements. Often, these experiences occur in solitude, in an ambiguous and unconstructed space. Consequently, the learner requires forms of control over processes and tools, especially during the difficult moments of inquiry verging on the edge of coherent knowledge. This requirements implies advisory services for learners, including supportive networks for referrals and exchanges. Some libraries are now providing outstanding environments for this kind of mediation. However, collaborative, helping voices are far less audible in museums.

Cultural institutions offer broad contexts and countless applications. The self-directed learner is often involved in the creation of meanings that go far beyond personal needs toward universality. Yet, most cultural institutions do not invite explorations of these meanings, nor do they provide useful opportunities for far-reaching dialogue. Though two separate self-directed learners can occupy a library or museum at the same time, they will remain distant from each other unless an accident causes their paths to cross. Consequently, the learner requires forms of connection and community, unobtrusive but available methods of communication with other inquirers. These methods could permit mutual, supportive discussions that serve to reduce isolation and to create an awareness of common processes. Adult independent learners do not have to suggest the image of untethered astronauts, each gazing at different points on the same horizon.

Several forms of nexus, mainly exchanges and brokerages, have been discussed and demonstrated for such untethered learners (Brookfield, 1983). While cultural institutions certainly ought to invest in existing networks for learners, I think that the more profitable investment lies in assisting the general adult public to understand itself as a community of learners, as people constantly making choices and learning from them. One way for a cultural institution to accomplish this purpose is to offer its adult users instructive reflections of themselves as learners. In case studies and personal narratives, adults can find mirrors of process and experience. In these places, as nowhere else, learners can become models for themselves and for each other. The institution might thereby easily communicate to its users that it offers a nurturant environment for inquirers.

Tools and Initiatives for Self-Direction in Cultural Institutions

Wherever they evolve, useful environments for self-directed learning depend on the imaginations of designers and on the needs of users, both of whom should come to understand how direct experiences, personal controls, and pervasive continuities occur in one learning life. Both libraries and museums have excellent, active professional organizations, several fine journals in which innovations are reported and dialogues are sustained, and cadres of thoughtful, devoted professionals. Two recent publications confirm this vitality: Zipporah Collins's (1981) excellent anthology and the spring 1983 issue of *Library Trends* (Burge, 1983). A third important item (Hoth, 1978), a sourcebook published by the Center for Museum Education, is available in microform.

Several inspiring indicators are worth describing here to suggest some elements of an ideal design for self-direction in cultural institutions. These few notes must stand for the many forms of attention that museums across the country are giving to adult learners.

At the National Museum of Natural History (Washington, D.C.), the Naturalist Center—a collection of 25,000 accessible specimens, library resources, microscopes, and other research instruments—assists adults to conduct independent inquiries in all disciplines supported by the museum.

At the Metropolitan Museum of Art (New York), the Ruth and Harold D. Uris Center for Education introduces museum users to its vast collections by means of thematic exhibits drawn from several areas, an introductory slide presentation, and a library and resource center available for public research.

The American Museum of Natural History (New York) offers useful free documentation to an important permanent exhibit, the Gardner D. Stout Hall of Asian Peoples. At the Metropolitan Museum, the recently enlarged Lila Acheson Wallace Galleries of Egyptian Art are documented, dynasty by dynasty, in a colorful brochure. (It is worth noting that study desks and sturdy chairs appear throughout these incomparable Metropolitan galleries.) Each of these galleries is a useful introduction to systematic inquiry and represents inviting documentation available widely in American museums.

At the Exploratorium (San Francisco), approximately seventy young adults are employed as "explainers." Their job is to assist visitors, explain physical principles, and participate in the development of exhibits. They help to achieve what the Exploratorium's founder, Frank Oppenheimer (1982, p. 42), has described as a balance "between unfettered exploration and detailed guidance."

Despite its 600 pages, a recent book by Adelheid M. Gealt (1983) can easily be carried about in any art museum. It offers taxonomies, maps, exemplary sketches and plates, historical data, and a bibliography. We need similar books about ways to learn from objects in museums of science and history.

Ronald Gross (1982, Gross and Gross, 1983) has documented both proved and potential contributions of cultural institutions to the work of self-directed learners. Gross (1982) is an inviting, supportive tool; Gross and Gross (1983) is a brief but stimulating report. Both works have valuable bibliographies and directories. These are early strides to fulfill the immense need for information about learning resources, which K. Patricia Cross (1978) has cogently documented. Allen Tough's (1980) small "pocket book for personal change" usefully addresses the adult's generic need for enriching personal knowledge.

All these works invite the learner to act for learning or assist the learner to construe independent ideas from accessible contents of first hand experiences. Moreover, although powerful technologies are available in cultural institutions, they do not appear to be independent of texts or helpers. In the age of information technology, it is important to say that human beings and written texts continue to play vital roles for learners in cultural institutions.

An inviting institution offers ideal mediation in several ways. In every community of learners we might envision a consortium of enlightened cultural educational services comprising public helpers, access to diverse reference tools and other texts, opportunities to examine specimens or consult subject specialists, and shopping areas in which inexpensive tools or examples could be purchased, rented, or borrowed for home study. These consortia would assist in the evolution of good questions, encourage appropriate literacies, facilitate dialogue and documentation among self-directed inquirers, help learners to overcome the inevitable obstacles and impasses, and invite extensive encounters with real things "on the horizons of our thoughts" (Kelly, 1977, p. 6). Large consortia are not necessary. One insightful agent in a library or museum is enough to cause important changes in how adult learners are assisted there. Wherever an individual or an institution has articulated a public agenda for education, the clarity of those inviting horizons has been enhanced.

References

Bateson, G. *Steps to an Ecology of Mind.* New York: Ballantine Books, 1972.

Boulding, K. E. "The Role of the Museum in the Propagation of Developed Images." *Technology and Culture,* 1966, *7* (1), 64–66.

Brookfield, S. *Adult Learners, Adult Education, and the Community.* New York: Teachers College Press, 1983.

Bruner, J. S. *Beyond the Information Given.* New York: Norton, 1973.

Burge, E. J. (Ed.). "Adult Learners, Learning, and Public Libraries." *Library Trends,* 1983, *31* (4), (entire issue).

Collins, Z. W. (Ed). *Museums, Adults, and the Humanities: A Guide for Educational Programming.* Washington, D.C.: American Association of Museums, 1981.

Cross, K. P. *The Missing Link: Connecting Adult Learners to Learning Resources.* New York: College Entrance Examination Board, 1978.

Gealt, A. M. *Looking at Art: A Visitor's Guide to Museum Collections.* New York: Bowker, 1983.

Gross, R. *The Independent Scholar's Handbook.* Reading, Mass.: Addison-Wesley, 1982.

Gross, R., and Gross, B. *Independent Scholarship: Promise, Problems, and Prospects.* New York: College Entrance Examination Board, 1983.

Hoth, S. R. (Ed.). *Lifelong Learning/Adult Audiences.* Washington, D.C.: Center for Museum Education, 1978. (ED 191 754)

Kelly, G. A. *A Theory of Personality: The Psychology of Personal Constructs.* New York: Norton, 1963.

Kelly G. A. "The Psychology of the Unknown." In D. Bannister (Ed.), *New Perspectives in Personal Construct Theory.* New York: Academic Press, 1977.

Lipton, B. "John Cotton Dana and the Newark Museum." *The Newark Museum Quarterly,* 1979, *30* (2–3) (entire issue).

Low, T. L. *The Museum as a Social Instrument.* New York: Metropolitan Museum of Art, American Association of Museums, 1942.

Oppenheimer, F. "Exploration and Culture." *Museum News,* 1982, *61* (2), 36–45.

Polanyi, M. *Personal Knowledge.* Chicago: University of Chicago Press, 1958.

Smith, R. M. *Learning How to Learn: Applied Theory for Adults.* New York: Cambridge Book, 1982.

Smith, R. M. (Ed.). *Helping Adults Learn How to Learn.* New Directions for Continuing Education, no. 19. San Francisco: Jossey-Bass, 1983.

Tough, A. M. *Expand Your Life: A Pocket Book for Personal Change.* New York: College Board, 1980.

Valery, P. *Aesthetics.* New York: Pantheon, 1964.

David Carr is associate professor at the Graduate School of Education, Rutgers–The State University of New Jersey, where he teaches about cultural institutions and lifelong learning.
A grant from the Rutgers University Research Council and the cooperation of the Education Department at the American Museum of Natural History assisted him in his recent work on thinking and learning in American cultural institutions.

Hospital orientation and in-service education programs for nurses are incorporating principles of self-directed learning into program design.

Applying Principles of Self-Directed Learning in the Health Professions

Carol Reed Ash

The use of self-directed learning in the health professions has been increasing in recent years. Various approaches have been incorporated into generic and graduate programs of study as well as into continuing education offerings and staff development programs in hospital settings. The rising cost of health care, the rapidly expanding use of sophisticated technologies, and increase in complex treatment protocols are changing the health care system and serving as catalysts for change in educational approaches. The very nature of the way in which professionals, such as physicians and nurses, function and the lives they affect as a result of their practice require them to possess a high degree of competence. Self-directed or autonomous learning must often be relied on in the development of such competence because of the differences in the needs of individual practitioners for information and in the time frame in which such information must be obtained.

Nursing is mandated to provide orientation and in-service education to those employed in a hospital setting, and good nursing requires education on a seven-days-a-week, twenty-four-hours-a-day continuum. This requirement challenges educators to be creative and innovative in developing programs to meet the needs of individual learners. In addition, the recent shortage of nurses

S. Brookfield (Ed.). *Self-Directed Learning: From Theory to Practice.* New Directions for Continuing Education, no. 25. San Francisco: Jossey-Bass, March 1985.

and some difficulty in retaining women in the profession have given new impetus to efforts to develop an alternate approach to the traditional lecture format historically used in nursing education. This chapter reviews self-directed training initiatives for nursing education in hospitals across the United States and describes in detail the application of self-directed learning principles to an orientation and in-service education program for nurses at one specific setting. It directs attention to the differences between self-directed learning as defined by Tough (1979) and self-directed learning as a process that an individual uses to accomplish program objectives defined by a nursing education department within the broad context of an organizational setting.

Trends in Self-Directed Learning

Orientation and in-service education programs for nurses serve two different groups of practitioners. Orientation programs are designed to reflect the American Nurses Association (1978) definition of such programs as introducing new staff members to the philosophy, goals, and procedures necessary to work in a particular setting. Orientation should also be provided to employees when they change roles and responsibilities. Under the American Nurses Association (1978) definition, in-service education programs are provided in the work setting to assist staff to perform assigned functions in the agency. The learning experiences may or may not be formally planned and evaluated, and they may include various approaches to learning.

Numerous program designs have been used to provide orientation. Many incorporate the principles of self-directed learning. Different approaches are described by del Bueno and others (1981), Martin (1979), Moran (1980), Rantz (1980), Schmidt and Quaife (1974), and Stopera and Scully (1974).

The competence-based education recommended by del Bueno and others (1981) emphasizes outcomes or achievement of performance expectations, self-directed learning, a flexible time frame for completion, the teacher as a facilitator, building on previous experiences, and assessing the individual as a learner. This approach is intended to hold down the escalating cost of traditional orientation programs and to free instructors from the classroom so they can be available to assist experienced staff in the patient units.

Brown (1978) describes a distinctive approach to staff orientation at the University of Washington Hospital. The program was implemented in response to a commitment that continuing education should be the philosophical foundation of the education department. The orientation program uses a centralized approach, with new staff developing individual programs and contracting for study time and relevant experiences. A learning resource center, self-directed learning modules, and the education staff, who serve as facilitators for individual learning, form the nucleus of available options and resources.

A clinical management model approach to education, as described by Martin (1979), provides a meaningful, systematic tool for management development. The model provides for orientation of employees to standards of care, patient outcomes, documentation guidelines, discharge planning, and patient teaching. Identification of a patient population, preparation of outcome criteria, development of general standards of care and of standards for documentation, evaluation of staff educational needs based on the patient population selected, and selection of appropriate health teaching information for the patient population are the focus of the core curriculum.

Moran (1980) stresses the need for individualizing the orientation of staff nurses. Emphasizing the learning needs and learning styles that each nurse brings to the orientation process, she emphasizes the redundancy and inadequacy of the traditional program, which cannot accommodate individual differences.

The modular approach described by Rantz (1980) divides content into twelve sections. The head nurse assumes major responsibility for the program, evaluating the progress of participants through the sections as each participant works first as a member of the team, then as a team leader. The goal of this approach is progressively to add the information necessary to function independently and capably.

Schmidt and Quaife (1974) describe orientation by contract. The orientee enters into a contract with the agency for completion of one set of experiences before proceeding to the next. This approach emphasizes self-direction, mutual negotiation, and mutual evaluation. The contract is negotiated between the employee and the instructor. It can be flexible in terms of time frame, although all standards must be met.

Stopera and Scully (1974) report a problem-solving approach that uses assessment, identification of the problem solution, implementation, and evaluation as a prescriptive educational program that relies on continuing education principles and teaching by objectives. Instructors carry a caseload of new employees assigned according to clinical areas. It is felt that this approach allows for individualization of learning needs at the time of entry into the hospital system.

As an adjunct to the orientation process, a number of hospitals now offer a preceptor program. A preceptor is a staff nurse selected to provide support to the new employee who is being oriented to the patient care unit. The preceptor assists the new employee to become increasingly more independent and self-directed in identifying learning needs and in delivering patient care. While the concept is not a new one, it has gained popularity in recent years.

Friesen and Conahan (1980), Murphy and Hammerstad (1981), and Plasse and Lederer (1981) describe similar approaches to the use of preceptors. In most instances, the preceptor serves as a role model and works with the new employee on a one-to-one basis. The preceptor is selected for his or her demonstrated clinical competence, good communication skills, and potential for career growth. The success of the preceptor approach is directly related to the careful selection of the preceptors and to the quality of the training program provided to those selected. Understanding orientation methods, teaching and learning principles, assessment of individual needs, and giving and receiving feedback are necessary content areas to be covered. A preceptor program offers the experienced staff nurse an opportunity for increased job satisfaction and professional growth. It also has the advantage of providing a support mechanism for new nursing graduates.

Self-directed in-service programs developed specifically to address the needs of the experienced staff nurse and to provide ongoing education once orientation is completed are not currently reported in the literature. Because of the large number of nurses who require in-service programs in order to maintain their clinical competence in the work setting, this area of program development represents one of the greatest challenges in hospital education for nurses today.

Orientation for Nursing Through Self-Direction

Continuing education provides the nursing education program described in this and the following sections with its philosophical foundation. A problem-centered approach to teaching, immediate application of knowledge, encouragement of self-directedness, acknowledgement of individual experience, and scheduling flexibility are the continuing education principles stressed in program design.

Program changes were initiated two years ago for Division of Nursing employees at Memorial Sloan-Kettering Cancer Center. The center is a 565-bed acute care hospital located in New York City. It is committed to care of the patient with cancer, to cancer research, and to cancer education. Because of its specialty, the hospital is a training group for both medical and nursing practitioners from all parts of the world, and it is affiliated with numerous medical and nursing school programs.

The program has three major components: a four-week orientation program for all nurses hired by the center, orientation programs of varying length for any member of the staff promoted or transferred to another position, and in-service programs designed to meet a variety of needs. The Department of Nursing Education, which I direct, is located within the Division of Nursing; it is responsible for the development, implementation, and evaluation of the overall program.

The process for designing and operating particular learning activities is based on the principles of andragogy (Knowles, 1980) which provide the rationale for program planning, curriculum development, teaching strategies, and program evaluation. The department believes that nurses are professionals capable of becoming more self-directed who bring to each learning experience varying, individually accumulated experiences and a desire to learn how to function in a rapidly changing and highly complex environment. A fundamental belief is that the immediate application of what is learned to performance in the clinical areas benefits both the individual practitioner and the patient.

The four-week orientation program for new nurses was the first part of the overall program to be revised, and revision served as the catalyst for change. Because this program is directed to the needs of a specific group of people at a particular point in time—entry into the organization—it was felt this would be the most advantageous way of beginning to introduce the principles of continuing education to a professional staff of approximately seven hundred registered professional nurses with varying academic backgrounds, varying years of experience, and little if any knowledge of these principles. The program is still in transition. Nevertheless, it is clear that a very traditional, lecture-oriented approach to educational programming is gradually being replaced by a more self-directed approach to learning.

Applying Self-Directed Strategies at Sloan-Kettering

For purposes of making self-directed learning an option for learners in an organizational setting, Tough's (1979) definition was used. That definition stipulates that self-directed learning is intentional rather than accidental or incidental, that acquiring definite knowledge or skill is the purpose of the activity, and that learning is to be retained over time. This definition is congruent with the definition used by the nursing profession for orientation and in-service education programs. As already noted, the American Nurses Association (1978) defines orientation as the process used to introduce new staff members and staff members who are changing roles and responsibilities to the philosophy, goals, policies, procedures, role expectations, physical facilities, and special services in a specific work setting. In-service education comprises the learning experiences conducted in the work setting to assist staff to function in a particular agency.

The major changes introduced into the traditional mode by the Sloan-Kettering self-directed program are reflected in the areas of program design, teaching strategies, and evaluation. Curriculum development remains an ongoing process and follows the essential concepts common to all program development (Boyle, 1981). The program design, teaching strategies, and evaluation methods developed for the four-week orientation are gradually being incorporated into the other programs.

The design of the program was the most critical aspect to resolve, because we believed it was the design that would foster self-directed learning. Approximately two hundred nurses must complete the program, which is conducted the first of every month. It is essential for all members of the nursing division to understand the program process so that time planning and patient care assignments can be managed.

Assessment of learner knowledge of continuing education and introduction of continuing education principles are integrated on the first day of the program with an explanation of the program and review of the criteria for completion. An orientation blueprint presented in chart format identifies the knowledge and skills required. This blueprint lists the resources that are available for each content area identified, it provides space for documentation after each learning activity is completed, it specifies the evaluation criteria, and it indicates how and by whom learning will be evaluated. The blueprint is introduced at the beginning of each program. In addition to being a tool that guides each learner through the orientation process, the blueprint is used to document the experiences acquired, and it becomes part of the personnel profile.

The resources identified represent the most significant change in teaching strategies. Most formal lecture presentations have been removed from the program. Self-instructional modules, videotape and sound-slide programs, films, reference manuals, performance checklists, selected readings, workshops, and individuals comprise the resources available for learners seeking to acquire needed knowledge and skills. The learner's time is divided between acquiring information and applying that information in the clinical area. Blocks of self-directed learning time included in the program schedule allow learners to select one of the content areas to complete; learners may also choose to spend the time in some other way.

A skills laboratory for problem-based learning uses clinical simulations as a means of validating psychomotor skills. A media resource room houses the audiovisual hardware and software; it is available to learners twenty-four hours a day. In addition, self-instructional modules are catalogued in the library and available for overnight loan. Learning is individualized, participative, and proactive, and it uses a variety of methods. It is problem- or patient-centered.

Participants are expected to complete the program within a reasonable time frame, and it is expected that clinical time will not be used as a substitute for the time needed to acquire information. Although the actual time depends on the individual learner's level of experience, it takes approximately four weeks to complete the program requirements. Clinical supervision is provided by both clinical instructors and preceptors. Each instructor is responsible for facilitating the educational process for learners in several clinical areas and serves as the primary resource throughout the orientation period. Preceptors are staff nurses who have been selected according to designated criteria and who have attended a workshop that introduces them to the principles of continuing education and the orientation process. Every orientee is assigned a preceptor for the duration of the orientation program. The preceptor provides additional educational support and facilitates learning in the clinical area.

Evaluation criteria combine demonstrations of competence, participation in workshops that use discussion and case study to assess knowledge, worksheets submitted to instructors, documentation on patient records, and exams in required areas.

An orientation blueprint has been developed for each clinical area and for each position in the Division of Nursing. The blueprint serves as a guide to identifying and developing the resources necessary for learners to acquire the information needed, and it provides the learner with a tool to facilitate the learning process. It also assists management personnel with the evaluation of individual performance, and it documents the educational process mandated both by the organization and by the Joint Commission on Accreditation of Hospitals.

A self-directed approach to in-service education is gradually being implemented through the use of preceptor training workshops and the use of an employee development record. A noticeable domino effect has occurred as new employees have completed the initial orientation program with an understanding of the principles of continuing education.

The Problems Encountered

The problems encountered in attempting to apply self-directed learning principles to a hospital-based nursing education program can be addressed in terms of program implementation, program design, faculty development, and financial considerations. The problems encountered in developing the Sloan-Kettering program are discussed here, along with recommendations by Reed (1984) for developing a new instructional delivery system for a hospital orientation and in-service education program.

Program Implementation. Implementing a new program in any organizational setting requires an understanding of the dynamics of planned change. Without a clear understanding of the organization and of the interpersonal relationships of those within it, change may not be possible. A nursing education department located within a division of nursing should be able to build in a measure of self-directedness without risk of institutional constraint. The position of the education department within the broad context of the organizational setting is the key to understanding how change should be initiated.

Resistance to implementation of this particular program was minimal, because of the general frustration and dissatisfaction with the previous system of orientation and in-service education and the general agreement that another approach might be advantageous. The readiness for change was apparent. Consultants and workshops conducted for administrative and key clinical personnel introduced the philosophy of continuing education as the theoretical framework for educational programming. It was recognized that it would take time to implement any new approach and that the education program would be in transition for several years. Support from nursing administrators is essential, since it validates that the department is prepared to change. Without it, the program environment will not be conducive to the facilitation of learning, and the program will be set up for failure.

Student reaction to being asked to become more self-directed has ranged from no reaction at all, to hesitant, to quite positive. Initial assessment reveals that most learners have never heard the term *adult education*. Of the approximately three hundred nurses who have completed the program thus far, about two thirds had never heard of self-directed learning. One third were familiar with the term, and they had been self-directed in acquiring various psychomotor skills.

The immediate problem that must be overcome lies in introducing the philosophy and the self-directed approach so that the learners feel they can begin to function. They adapt to the approach in varying ways. Some require no assistance at all. Others require assistance from both the instructor and the preceptor on a daily basis. That some will require more assistance than others and a longer time period to complete the orientation program is anticipated. The program design must be flexible enough to be responsive to individual need, but it cannot be so flexible that it allows freedom to complete at any time. Organizational constraints of ensuring adequate staff to deliver patient care services must be recognized.

When the employee begins the program, there is an initial period of confusion until everyone becomes comfortable with the self-directed process. Learning resources must be available. Enormous frustration is created when self-direction is required but the self-directed person is unable to accomplish objectives because resources have been misplaced or because not enough copies of the self-instructional modules are available. A negative initial experience with self-directed learning discourages the learner from continuing the process for further orientation and in-service education.

Some groups of nurses need continued reinforcement about how to function as self-directed learners, particularly if the concepts are new to the entire group. In some instances, a sense of freedom and procrastination result in poor use or no use of self-directed time, and the result is failure to comply with program objectives. Group discussion of organizational expectations, of professional accountability, and of the parameters of self-directed learning often clarifies misconceptions, stimulates learners to proceed, and facilitates completion of the orientation process.

Program Design. Designing a program that incorporates continuing education principles and that encourages learners to be self-directed creates problems not usually encountered when designing a program based on the traditional lecture or conference approach. The process of designing alternate learning strategies produces a variety of learning experiences to which the learner must have direct access. The amount of time that it takes to change from lecture program design to a design that uses a variety of instructional strategies must be anticipated by the faculty and all members of the nursing division.

The expertise required to develop the learning materials must also be anticipated. Unless the department has access to instructional design personnel and the budget to develop various audiovisual software programs, there may be a tendency to develop only self-instructional modules. Various teaching strategies must be considered, and creativity in the development of various instructional approaches must be encouraged.

As the instructional programs are developed, space must be provided to house the materials, and a system to maintain the educational materials must be developed. A media resource room facilitates access by organizing the educational materials in one central place, and a learning resource manual lists all available educational software, identifies the hardware required, and indicates the time required for each program. The manual is a key element in orienting the entire nursing staff to individualized learning, and it facilitates introduction of the self-directed concept. Lack of a thoughtful and workable plan will cause disorganization when the program is initiated that can frustrate the learner and discourage acceptance of the concept.

Extending the continuing education program design to in-service education is not as easy as extending it to orientation. In-service education must be available twenty-four hours a day seven days a week, and it must meet the needs of the largest percentage of the nursing staff requiring education at any given time. Differences in academic preparation and experience are extreme, and relatively few staff members are familiar with the self-directed concept. However, as Cooper (1980) points out, nursing practice has changed so dramatically in the last twenty-five years that a formal, organized approach to education will not address the needs of the individual practitioner. Self-directed learning appears to be essential to the continued provision of quality patient care services.

If the education staff responsible and accountable for orientation are also responsible and accountable for in-service education, then a coordinated, integrated approach is easier to implement than if they are not. Unless there is a direct line of responsibility from the clinical area to the education area, approaches to the provision of learning for staff who have completed the orientation program may be fragmented. Once the transition has been made to a continuing education framework for all programs, it is easier to strengthen the various educational efforts required in the clinical area.

Evaluation methodology remains one of the most difficult areas to address when implementing a self-directed educational program in an organizational setting. Some testing mechanisms must remain in place to satisfy hospital accreditation criteria. Evaluation that documents clinical competence and thus the quality of a nurse's work is the most significant. As standards for patient care continue to be developed and as clinical performance is assessed through quality assurance programs, the impact of the self-directed approach on hospital education can better be evaluated. Whether the traditional or the self-directed approach has the better effect on the quality of work is as yet unknown. Assessing the respective merits of these two approaches is one of nursing education's greatest needs and challenges.

Faculty Development. Faculty development and faculty orientation to continuing education constitute the first essential step in developing a new program. Most nurse educators in the hospital setting have not been exposed to continuing education philosophy as part of their generic and graduate education. Therefore, staff in the program must be committed to change, and they must understand the various aspects of the proposed changes in the program design.

Consultative and in-service efforts that encourage faculty to broaden their instructional techniques and that place an emphasis on independent learning will assist each faculty member to become less insecure as lecture content is offered in some other way. During the development of the Sloan-Kettering program, faculty expressed frustration because they were unsure that what they were doing was correct. Their initial hesitancy in assuming the role of facilitator gave way to overwhelming enthusiasm for the role as each one experienced the transition. During the initial phase, weekly departmental in-service education programs provided staff with an opportunity to discuss problems with one another. Instructors identified specific areas of need, such as teaching strategies, and consultants provided additional support in those areas and facilitated the understanding needed to initiate program changes.

Financial Considerations. Questions regarding the cost of implementing any new program and assessment of whether the new program is more cost-effective than the old one are critical in health care education today. There is no definitive answer for the Sloan-Kettering program. It is obvious that the instructors and preceptors now function in a different way. The instructors spend less time in the classroom and more time in the clinical area, and they are more available as an immediate resource and role model. The preceptors are more comfortable as a result of training workshops, and they understand the orientation process better, with the result that there is less confusion, and the relationship between orientees and preceptors is stronger.

Initial costs for program development and the purchase of audiovisual hardware and software must be anticipated. Once the program is in place, however, such expenditures should decrease. The question that must be raised is whether the increased use of human resources, as a program of this design seems to require, and the financial investment necessary to implement the program are justified by improved learner outcomes. Is the cost in dollars and cents greater? Does a self-directed program enhance the quality of patient care, and does it promote the recruitment and retention of staff? A comparative analysis of the costs of a traditional lecture approach to programming and the program described here can provide some answers. It is essential, however, for the other issues to be addressed if nursing service administrators are to support the self-directed approach as a viable alternative to a lecture-oriented approach.

The Future

A hospital-based orientation and in-service education program that incorporates the principles of continuing education, that emphasizes individualization, and that encourages self-directed learning can be implemented as described here. Learners at Sloan-Kettering are responding positively to the approach, and they appear to be more motivated to acquire additional skills and knowledge through in-service education.

There is evidence that continuing education is being accepted by nurse educators as the way of the future. What that means for program design is unknown. We do not know whether a single approach is applicable to all settings, and we do not know whether we are all talking about the same thing when we use the term *self-directed*. Indeed, if we define self-directed learning as something that occurs when adults are involved in the planning, conduct, and evaluation of their own learning, is such learning possible in a hospital setting? In a situation where what must be learned is prescribed by professional and organizational constraints, is the learner self-directed in the full meaning of the term, or is a distorted, constrained form of self-direction in operation? If a continuing education approach and the use of self-directed learning are to succeed in nursing education, terms must be clarified to avoid frustrating learners and to promote the continuing development of what appears to be a very exciting and important trend for nurse educators.

References

American Nurses Association. *Guidelines for Staff Development.* Monograph COE–11 SM. Kansas City, Mo.: American Nurses Association, 1978.

Boyle, P. G. *Planning Better Programs.* New York: McGraw-Hill, 1981.

Brown, J. B. (Ed.). "On The Scene: Staff Development at University Hospital, University of Washington." *Nursing Administration Quarterly,* 1978, *2* (2), 11–52.

Cooper, S. S. (Ed.). *Self-Directed Learning in Nursing.* Wakefield, Mass.: Nursing Resources, 1980.

del Bueno, D. J., Barker, F., and Christmyer, C. "Implementing a Competency-Based Orientation Program." *Journal of Nursing Administration,* 1981, February, 24–29.

Friesen, L., and Conahan, B. J. "A Clinical Preceptor Program: Strategy for New Graduate Orientation." *Journal of Nursing Administration,* 1980, April, 18–23.

Knowles, M. *The Modern Practice of Adult Education.* New York: Cambridge Book, 1980.

Martin, N. S. "Clinical Management Models: Staff Education Curriculum for Quality Assurance." *Supervisor Nurse,* 1979, *10* (119), 24–28.

Moran, V. "Notes on Continuing Education." *Journal of Continuing Education in Nursing,* 1980, *11* (2), 54–59.

Murphy, M. L., and Hammerstad, S. M. "Preparing a Staff Nurse for Precepting." *Nurse Educator,* 1981, September-October, 17–20.

Plasse, N. J., and Lederer, J. R. "Preceptors—A Resource for New Nurses." *Journal for Nursing Leadership and Management,* 1981, June, 35–41.

Rantz, M. J. "A Modular Approach to Unit Orientation." *Supervisor Nurse,* 1980, *11* (6), 48–51.

Reed, C. A. "Staff Development for Nurses: A Nontraditional Approach." Unpublished doctoral dissertation, Columbia University, 1984.

Schmidt, M. C., and Quaife, M. C. "Orientation by Contract." *Supervisor Nurse,* 1974, *5* (10), 35–39, 43–44.

Stopera, V., and Scully, V. "A Staff Development Model." *Nursing Outlook,* 1974, *22* (6), 390–393.

Tough, A. *The Adult's Learning Projects: A Fresh Approach to Theory and Practice in Adult Learning.* (2nd ed.) Austin, Texas: Learning Concepts, 1979.

Carol Reed Ash is director of nursing education at Memorial Sloan-Kettering Cancer Center in New York City and editor of Cancer Nursing: An International Journal for Cancer Care.

Professional continuing educators working in institutional settings can find ways of supporting the activities of informal, self-directed learners.

The Continuing Educator and Self-Directed Learning in the Community

Stephen Brookfield

As professions develop, they tend to present themselves as guardians of some kinds of secret knowledge or skill too sophisticated for the layperson to appreciate. This has occurred most vividly with the legal and medical professions, both of which are perceived by the general public as dealing in language and as exhibiting skills far beyond the purview of any "ordinary" person. Such a perception works to the great economic advantage of the professionals concerned, since they can charge high fees to laypersons who need legal or medical services.

Recently, however, there have been challenges to the idea that members of accredited professions control skills possessed only by a select few. Experiments in alternative legal services, free legal aid centers, the growth of interest in holistic medicine, and the increasing practice of home remedy, self-help medicine all indicate that the position of privilege and prestige occupied by professionals is being regarded with growing skepticism.

Much the same trend can be observed in continuing education. In recent years, continuing educators have sought the mantle of professionalism partly in reaction to their perceived position of marginality with regard to the rest of the educational system. In contrast to the years between the two world

S. Brookfield (Ed.). *Self-Directed Learning: From Theory to Practice.* New Directions for Continuing Education, no. 25. San Francisco: Jossey-Bass, March 1985.

wars and the decades of the 1940s and 1950s, when the traditions of community development and social activism were dear to the hearts of continuing educators, the professional continuing educator is seen today as a master technician of learning who works within a formal institution.

Moreover, those who work in today's educational institutions as continuing educators are concerned with running programs on a cost-recovery or profit basis. Such an ethos displays little sympathy for the adults who choose to ignore formal educational institutions and who conduct learning efforts on their own. Thus, it is not surprising to find the keynote speaker at the 1981 national convention of the Adult Education Association of the United States declaring that independent learners are the "competition" to continuing education.

In this era of reduced public funding for education, when continuing educators everywhere are struggling to maintain their programs, why, it might be asked, should we bother to concern ourselves with assisting adult learners who ignore formal programs? This question is even more pertinent when we realize that adults seem to undertake considerable amounts of learning on their own (Tough, 1979; Penland, 1979), often to sophisticated levels of expertise (Brookfield, 1981). Just as recipients of legal and medical services are choosing to devise strategies allowing them to deal with legal and medical problems without calling for the aid of expensive professionals, so our clients, adult learners, are choosing to design and conduct their own educational experiences.

Professional Educators and Self-Directed Learners

There is a host of reasons why professional continuing educators should not view independent learners as irrelevant or competitive to their work. At a very basic ethical level, educators have a moral duty to try to assist those engaged in learning wherever and whenever the opportunity arises. Just as medical doctors are enjoined by the Hippocratic oath to cure illness regardless of the patient's race, class, or nationality, so educators are ethically bound to aid those individuals engaged in learning irrespective of their location or characteristics.

Second, the research of Tough (1979) and Brookfield (1981) has demonstrated that adults who are learning outside of formal institutions are not engaged in some defiant act of rejection. Repeatedly, such adults declare that they would like more help from the formal sector with their learning efforts and that their decision to learn independently was due to a lack of suitable course offerings at their local continuing education center.

Third, the research of Tough (1979) and Houle (1961) has shown that adults frequently intersperse their self-directed pursuit of learning with enrollment in formally provided continuing education courses. Learners who receive assistance in their self-directed efforts from professional continuing educators are likely to turn to the same educators when the time for course participation arises.

Fourth, the professionals who assist individuals and groups of adults engaged in learning outside of formal settings are undertaking valuable trust-building public relations endeavors. Studies of participation in adult education attest to the importance of word-of-mouth recommendations as motivators for adults to attend classes. The professional who works with self-directed learners is raising the profile of the local continuing education program in the minds of adults in the area.

Fifth, as the next section of this chapter demonstrates, it is sometimes possible, by some form of institutional innovation, to make an arrangement that allows self-directed learners to maintain control over their learning but to become affiliated with a local providing institution. Mechanisms for the assessment of prior experiential learning and open learning centers are examples of institutional adaptation and innovation that have worked to the benefit of self-directed learners.

Sixth, there is broad societal justification for continuing educators to become more actively involved in the efforts of self-directed learners. If such phrases as *lifelong education* and *the learning society* are to possess any meaning beyond that which they have when they are ritually invoked at conference gatherings, then professional educators must become crucially involved in assisting self-directed learners. It is impossible to conceive of a lifelong education system that does not have some provision for assisting self-directed learners as a central component. Such a commitment was recognized in a recent policy outline undertaken by the British Advisory Council for Adult and Continuing Education (ACACE) (1982), which called for a network of well-staffed centers of independent learning housed in public libraries.

Finally, it is in the democratic interest of any society to have as many adults as possible engaged in creative, self-directed learning. It is a truism that the creative talents of its citizenry is a society's most valuable asset, its greatest resource. If this is so, then it is in a society's political and economic interest to ensure that as many of its members as can be arranged are engaged in learning at any one time. A citizenry that is actively involved in learning is likely to be politically literate and to be open to the kinds of retraining and adaptation required by technological change. A society composed of inquiring, questing adults is one in which invention and innovation will flourish. Since formal structures will be unable to accommodate all these adults who wish to learn, substantial assistance will have to be granted by professionals working in those structures.

Supporting Self-Directed Learning in the Community: A Case Study

The paragraphs that follow document my attempts to work from within a formal continuing education setting with adults who chose to learn independently of that setting. These efforts took place in Malvern Hills College, a continuing education center in the West Midlands region of England. From 1974 to 1980, I was employed as a continuing education organizer at the college. My specific charge was to create innovative access points for those adults who traditionally avoided contact with the college.

The college was established in the wake of the Russell Report (Her Majesty's Stationery Office, 1973). That report called for innovative ways of involving disadvantaged adults in continuing education. In support of the report's injunctions, college policy was to emphasize the development of informal, community-based continuing education. In my particular department, the criteria of success were not to be found in class sizes or numbers of courses. Rather, we were to attempt to elicit the perceptions of groups and individuals in the local community regarding the educational experiences that they perceived as being most meaningful to them. Once we had gained an idea of these notions of significance, our task was to ensure that we as educators assisted such meaningful learning in whatever context and at whatever time it seemed most appropriate.

Before establishing any mechanisms to support such significant learning, it was obvious that we needed to gain as clear a picture as possible of the amount, nature, and variety of learning that was occurring within the community. To this end, a colleague and I conducted a community survey of local environments for adult learning and of the activities of local community groups that might exhibit an educational dimension. Much information was available as primary data collected by various agencies and deposited in the local public library. Surveys of the area had been conducted by voluntary groups and local industries and as educational projects. Taken along with the census data available for public consultation in all public libraries, these materials provided us with a reasonably accurate socioeconomic picture of the area.

As a means of coming to know something both of the range of learning environments and of the kinds of learning sponsored by local community groups in the region, we decided to interview members of local community groups. These interviews were to be conducted in the community settings in which the group was active. In this way, we would gain interview data and observational information about the purpose, content, and location of group-sponsored self-directed learning. We visited church halls, regional libraries, private homes, nurseries, pubs, schools, and other centers of activity and talked with clergy, voluntary society coordinators, local councillors, social workers, playgroup leaders, teachers, and community activists, among others. It cannot be denied that the information we received may have been biased, or personally distorted. However, given our time and labor constraints, consulting such individuals seemed to be the quickest, cheapest, and most convenient way of collecting initial information on the activities of local community groups, on the range and variety of settings for learning, and on the socioeconomic composition of the region.

There was a highly personal dimension to this process of community immersion and community study. Soon after arriving to take up my post, I joined the local social services department as a voluntary social worker. After accompanying a local social worker on her casework rounds, I was assigned to a particular case. Such experience could not masquerade as considered investigation of community characteristics, but it did bring home to me, in a personal and powerful manner, the kinds of problems that would typically confront certain groups of residents in the community.

An Educational Advisory Service for Adults

Having engaged in a preliminary investigation of community characteristics, learning environments, and group activities, we felt that it was now time to make some educational response to the educational needs that we felt had been revealed. The first such response took the form of an educational advisory service for adults. This service was established in order to help adults who wished to engage in some form of formal education to negotiate the maze of opportunities facing them. To this extent, the service functioned as something similar to an educational brokerage agency. As well as helping those who desired formal education to find their way through the bewildering maze of possibilities open to them, the service was concerned to assist adults in their pursuit of self-directed learning projects. Clients came to the service with an expressed desire to explore some new skill or knowledge area, and it was my function to suggest resource possibilities, to assist in the design of future learning, and to help with the practice of independent learning skills.

The educational advisory service was offered free to all members of the community. No distinction was made between prospective college (that is, continuing education center) students and those who were using the service with no thought of future enrollment in mind. The service was offered on a walk-in basis on one evening each week. No appointment was necessary. The service was available at other times during the week by appointment.

As the political and financial climate of the region and the country began to change, the service faced some criticism regarding its free nature and its availability to local community members who were not Malvern Hills college students. I argued that a local community center for continuing education was morally bound to make some effort to assist the learning of adults not formally enrolled in college courses. Such an argument based on ethical principles was received favorably when the service was introduced in a time of relatively beneficent public funding for education. By the time I left the college, however, it had become increasingly difficult to justify the moral necessity for continuation of the service to some public officials. Only because I was prepared to work well over my contractual work load was it allowed to continue. The marginality of the continuing educator who seeks to assist the informal learning efforts of adults will no doubt be familiar to many readers of this book. Further information on the establishment and functioning of the service can be found in Brookfield (1977a, 1983).

Home Study Service

In addition to the requests for assistance from adults who sought to conduct independent learning projects or to negotiate entry into some formal course of study, we received a number of requests for assistance with highly individualized learning efforts. The educational advisory service concerned itself with the development of general self-directed learning skills involving design, location of resources, and goal setting. However, some local learners wished for more individualized and ongoing assistance with a learning project that they were already conducting. These adults would typically already be working in a self-directed mode, but they preferred some kind of learning contact or consultant from whom they could obtain advice and with whom they could discuss possible learning alternatives.

The function of the home study service was to provide independent learners with such a learning partner. Some learners requested a degree of structure that required me to adopt a fairly didactic stance. When an adult said, "I really need you to indicate some introductory reading for me in sociology" or asked, "How do I get an idea of the central ideas of Freud?" there seemed little option other than to make a number of suggestions concerning fairly specific resources. As Mezirow suggests in Chapter Two of this volume, it is impossible to be a fully self-directed learner in a skill or knowledge area with which one is completely unfamiliar.

A critical feature of the service was an initial diagnostic interview at which learner and faculty member would discuss the learner's perceived needs. A negotiated learning contract arose from this initial meeting. The contract outlines a scheme of work, some specific objectives, and a timetable for the work in hand. Contracts typically were adjusted at least once during a semester period, often more frequently. Learners were always free to veto or renegotiate elements of the contract.

Four different kinds of program were requested: assistance with preparation for an examination or for entry into a formal course of study; assistance in exploring an area of skill or knowledge purely for its innate fascination and enjoyment; assistance in improving specific study skills, such as notetaking or essay planning; and assistance with the conduct of a specific, ongoing learning effort.

One defining characteristic of the service was the flexibility of time, place, and format of meetings subsequent to the initial interview. Such meetings were called *tutorials,* although there was often no formal, didactic transfer of information. We would meet in learners' homes, often on weekends or in the evenings, and we would be prepared to alter the negotiated work scheme as seemed appropriate. The critical features of the service were its flexibility, its working with clients in their own settings, its ceding of control over goals and objectives to learners, its emphasis on negotiation of all aspects of learning, and the college auspices under which this all occurred. The learners were enrolled as students in the college, and they paid a flat fee based on the number of hours of assistance they typically received from the tutor in charge of the service (myself). Auditing and administrative requirements meant that I had to use the terms *students* and *tutorials* in describing and documenting the service's operation. I also kept a "class" register of students' names and number of tutorials. In practice, however, meetings were off campus, subject to continual renegotiation, and conducted in a relaxed atmosphere. Flexibility of operation and recognition of the primacy of learners' needs were central to the service's operation. Further details on the service can be found in Brookfield (1977b, 1978a).

Return-to-Study Program

The educational advisory service and the home study service were both informal, individually oriented mechanisms for assisting self-directed learners. They were flexible in operation, they were cognizant of the primacy of learners' needs, and they consisted of individually negotiated learning programs. The home study service was home-based, and the educational advisory service was free of charge.

It became increasingly evident, however, that, while many adults preferred the relative privacy and individual orientation of the home study and educational advisory services, there were others who kept requesting some form of group learning effort. These adults wished to engage in purposeful learning of some kind, but they often had no specific skill or knowledge area in mind. What they felt they needed was some kind of group activity, with like-minded peers, that would prompt them to start thinking in some more systematic, inquiring manner than their work typically required. Such individuals would ring me up or arrive at the college asking for "a course to get me thinking again," "something to reactivate my brain cells," or "something to stop me from vegetating." However, they were unable to specify any particular content or skill area. Most wished to engage in formal study of some kind, but they felt they needed some form of prior learning activity to prepare them for formal study.

In response to this group of adults, a return-to-study program was established. This program centered on a series of return-to-study courses, which were offered throughout the year either as a series of eight to ten evening meetings or as single-weekend workshops. The content of the courses was more prescribed than it was in either of the two initiatives already discussed, although participants would introduce new topics or alter the sequence of topics. The sessions focused on developing the cognitive and affective skills considered necessary for successful study within formal educational settings. Cognitive skills of critical analysis, selectivity and discrimination in reading, essay planning, notetaking, and preparation for examinations were covered. Affectively, participation in discussion was encouraged so that adults entering seminar-based courses would not feel intimidated by the prospect of public speaking. In addition, an attempt was made to redress the poor self-image that these adults held of themselves as learners. Participants were encouraged to talk about the learning that they had undertaken by themselves over the past few years. In this way, they were encouraged to see themselves as already possessing some skills of goal setting, resource location, and information analysis. A session on adult learning discussed research that contradicted the view accepted by course members that their learning abilities diminished with age.

Although the return-to-study program consisted of courses and workshops run by an accredited educator, it can still be considered to have enhanced the self-directedness of adults in the local community. In effect, the object of the course was to assist these adults to develop their own nascent study skills so that they could be more confident about undertaking self-directed learning activities. The course was also concerned with enhancing participants' image of themselves as learners and with nurturing the confidence that they would need if they were to approach formal educational institutions for further study. Documentation of the program can be found in Brookfield (1978b), and the cognitive and affective problems experienced by adults attending these courses are discussed in Brookfield (1979a).

Supporting Autonomous Adult Learning Groups

The final initiative that I undertook to support self-directed learning in this community setting was community-based in every respect. I discovered from a woman who took a sociology course that I taught at the college each year that she was involved in a women's discussion group, which met in members' homes on alternate weeks. These women belonged to a network called the National Housewives Register (NHR), which existed to promote the discussion of nondomestic issues, primarily matters of social and political concern. I was invited to address the group one evening. There I discovered a thriving study circle engaged in eager discussion of such issues as the effects of television viewing, juvenile delinquency, children who were the products of divorce, and penal alternatives.

As a leader of adult discussion groups, I was only too aware of how easily they could become emotional battlegrounds or wandering exchanges of personal reminiscence. It seemed appropriate, therefore, to offer to the group some assistance in ensuring that their leaderless discussion sessions would be as meaningful and productive as possible. The idea was to introduce a modest analogue of the living room learning, study circle, and learning box schemes that were well documented in Sweden, North America, and Australia. The result was the Supporting Autonomous Adult Learning Groups scheme.

The scheme was simple. Several days before the group was to meet, the secretary collected a resource pack from me, which she then distributed to each of the group members. The resource pack, which I prepared, comprised four elements pertaining to the topic under examination: a sheet of relevant statistical data, extracts from relevant studies and reports, proposed alternative explanations for the phenomenon under discussion, and key questions suggesting topics that might be explored during the discussion.

The group was in control of the learning agenda and the learning activity. Its members provided me with a series of topics to be discussed on different evenings and collected the packages before each session. I was not present at the discussion sessions. Control of group goals, group process, and group location was entirely in the hands of group members. Although I selected the materials included in the packages, one had no sense that the content amounted to a prescribed curriculum. As I have noted in an account of the scheme (Brookfield, 1979b), the resource package was intended to minimize the risk that the discussions would meander; that participants would be intolerant of contrary, minority opinions; or that meetings would become emotional battlegrounds for the furtherance of individual self-esteem. If all members possessed some knowledge of the topic under scrutiny, it would be difficult for them to engage in diversionary strategems or to speak from positions of prejudice or ignorance.

Conclusion

The foregoing activities represent the efforts of one professional continuing educator to devise innovative ways of supporting the self-directed learning efforts of the adults in one local community. I do not anticipate that these activities can be replicated in a wide range of contrasting settings. Each educator must adapt to the circumstances, resources, and personal capabilities that he or she possesses.

What the preceding account indicates, perhaps, is that, even in the context of performing the traditional functions of planning programs and teaching courses, it is possible to make some kind of contact with informal, self-directed learners. Such contact does not need to be a saintly act of altruism on the part of the educator. Many clients of the various services just cited came to be regular attendees of more formally organized college courses. Viewed in this light, even the free educational advisory service came to be cost-effective in that it increased the commitment of clients to learning and in that that commitment became manifest in formal course participation. In the case of the home study service and the supporting autonomous adult learning group schemes, it was possible to arrange for participants to pay a fee to the college for the services that they were receiving.

It is widely attested that adult learners alternate periods of self-directed study with engagement in formal courses. Therefore, any efforts to assist them in periods of self-directed inquiry are likely to pay institutional dividends at a later date. It was not uncommon, for example, for clients of the educational advisory service to enroll in the home study service for an individualized study program or to take a return-to-study course. That circumstances or preferences sometimes dictate a temporary pursuit of learning in an individual mode clearly does not mean that all learning efforts in the individual's life will be conducted in that mode.

It would be remiss to close this account of one professional's attempts to work from within an institutional context to assist self-directed learners in the community without some mention of the stresses and strains induced by such efforts. I have written elsewhere of the limbo in which the informal continuing educator must operate and of the high tolerance for ambiguity required for such work (Brookfield, 1983). The informal continuing educator will remain professionally marginal most of the time. This marginality will alternate with occasional periods of institutional celebration, usually when the institution concerned is under attack for the elitist nature of the services that it provides. At such a time, the educator who works with groups not normally present in the college population will be presented to critics as an example of the college's innovative work. However, such institutional expressions of esteem are as a rule only temporary. When the attack is withdrawn, so is the visibility and prestige accorded the educator.

In such a situation, it is incumbent on the informal educator to develop a network of like-minded professionals. In my own case, I well remember the feeling of welcome professional solidarity that I experienced when I realized that my efforts to establish a home study service, an educational advisory service, and return-to-study courses were being paralleled at a number of other institutions. It was also useful to be able to call on colleagues in this network when my own program was under threat of dissolution.

The tale is not one primarily of overwork, however, or of acting on the defensive against predatory budget pruners. Attempts to help adult learners make their lives more personally meaningful tell a tale of pleasure and satisfaction. The expressions of genuine appreciation offered by adults for whom my efforts produced some kind of joy in learning more than compensated for the institutional neglect.

References

Advisory Council for Adult and Continuing Education. *Continuing Education: From Policies to Practice.* Leicester, England: Advisory Council for Adult and Continuing Education, 1982.

Brookfield, S. D. "Educational Advice for Adults." *Education and Training* (U.K.), 1977a, *19* (5), 137–139.

Brookfield, S. D. "A Local Correspondence Tuition Service." *Adult Education* (U.K.), 1977b, *50* (1), 39–43.

Brookfield, S. D. "Individualizing Adult Learning: An English Experiment." *Lifelong Learning: The Adult Years,* 1978a, *1* (7), 18–20.

Brookfield, S. D. "Learning to Learn: The Characteristics, Motivations, and Destinations of Adult Study Skills Students." *Adult Education* (U.K.), 1978b, *50* (6), 363–368.

Brookfield, S. D. "Adult Study Problems." *Journal of Further and Higher Education* (U.K.), 1979a, *3* (1), 91–96.

Brookfield, S. D. "Supporting Autonomous Adult Learning Groups." *Adult Education* (U.K.), 1979b, *51* (6), 366–369.

Brookfield, S. D. "Independent Adult Learning." *Studies in Adult Education,* 1981, *13* (1), 15–27.

Brookfield, S. D. *Adult Learners, Adult Education, and the Community.* New York: Teachers College Press, 1983.

Her Majesty's Stationery Office. *Adult Education: A Plan for Development.* London: Her Majesty's Stationery Office, 1973.

Houle, C. O. *The Inquiring Mind.* Madison: University of Wisconsin Press, 1961.

Penland, P. R. "Self-Initiated Learning." *Adult Education,* 1979, *29* (3), 170–179.

Tough, A. M. *The Adult's Learning Projects: A Fresh Approach to Theory and Practice in Adult Learning.* (2nd ed.) Austin, Texas: Learning Concepts, 1979.

Stephen Brookfield is assistant professor of adult and continuing education and associate director of the Center for Adult Education at Teachers College, Columbia University, New York City.

*This chapter reviews some useful sources for further inquiry
in self-directed learning theory and practice.*

Sources in Self-Directed Learning Theory and Practice

Stephen Brookfield

To supplement the chapters in this volume, this chapter suggests some sources
for further inquiry that will be useful to readers who wish to explore the field of
self-directed learning. The first section describes the chief reviews of research
in this area. The second section indicates the kinds of attempts that have been
made to translate the philosophy of self-direction into practical programs, processes, and curricula. My comments note the orientation and suitability of
these sources.

Research on Self-Directed Learning

Brookfield, S. K. *Independent Adult Learning.* Nottingham, England: Department of Adult Education, University of Nottingham, 1982.

A monograph in the *Adults: Psychological and Educational Perspectives* series, this
annotated bibliography describes the major British, American, and Canadian
research reports on self-directed learning. Topics include the nature of independent learning, providing support for independent learning, the methodology of the research into such learning, and directions for future research.

Penland, P. R. *Self-Planned Learning in America.* Pittsburgh: Graduate School
   of Library and Information Sciences, University of Pittsburgh, 1977.

S. Brookfield (Ed.). *Self-Directed Learning: From Theory to Practice.* New Directions
for Continuing Education, no. 25. San Francisco: Jossey-Bass, March 1985.

This is the only national survey to date of independent, self-directed learning. A national probability sample of 1,501 adults across the United States was interviewed regarding reasons for learning, preferred locations, and attitudes to this form of learning. The monograph concludes with a proposed self-directed learner's bill of rights.

Tough, A. M. *The Adult's Learning Projects: A Fresh Approach to Theory and Practice in Adult Learning.* (2nd ed.) Austin, Texas: Learning Concepts, 1979.

In this work, Allen Tough surveys his research into self-teaching, major learning efforts, and learning projects. The volume summarizes his early studies of self-teaching and reasons for conducting learning projects, which were conducted in the 1960s; it documents his subsequent researches, and a useful postscript reviews the efforts of other researchers during the 1970s. New data from a 1970 survey are also included. Tough concludes that 70 percent of learning efforts are self-planned, that almost all adults conduct one or two projects a year, and that adults commonly spend 700 hours pursuing learning projects. This volume is an essential reference work.

Practice in Self-Directed Learning

Boud, D. *Developing Student Autonomy in Learning.* New York: Nichols, 1981.

The contributors to this international anthology of readings represent England, New Zealand, Australia, Canada, and Switzerland. They review how learning contracts, independent study arrangements, and self-directed learning techniques have been introduced into higher education.

Brookfield, S. D. *Adult Learners, Adult Education, and the Community.* New York: Teachers College Press, 1983.

The author reviews the manner in which adults learn—in individual and group modes—without the assistance of professional educators. Part 1 summarizes research into self-directed learning and analyzes the nature of such learning. Part 2 documents how adults acquire skills and knowledge through involvement in community projects. Part 3 presents a number of case studies in which educators have worked to support self-directed learning in individual and group modes. Historical and contemporary case studies from America, Canada, and Britain are cited in analyses of the nature and variety of informal, self-directed learning.

Gross, R. *The Lifelong Learner.* New York: Simon & Schuster, 1979.

A book for the general, rather than academic, reader, this work contains a section on "The Invisible University" that provides a good review of sources and opportunities for self-directed learners, which range from libraries, learning exchanges, networks, churches, and television to cassettes, brokering agencies, games, and activist groups.

Gross, R. *The Independent Scholar's Handbook.* Reading, Mass.: Addison-Wesley, 1982.

A practical handbook to assist those who wish to undertake a sustained, independent exploration of a field of interest, this work explores the intellectual histories of individual scholars and documents group supports that can further such scholarship. The book is crammed with anecdotes and suggestions for activity.

Houle, C. O. *Patterns of Learning: New Perspectives on Life-Span Education.* San Francisco: Jossey-Bass, 1984.

A highly personal, biographical analysis of the great men (no women are discussed at length) of independent learning—Montaigne, Pope, Thoreau, Everett, Osler, and (surprising to some no doubt) Billy Graham. Houle argues that Florence can be viewed as a center of culture and shows how scholars and artists through the centuries have used its resources. The chapters arguing for a variety of learning patterns, critiquing traditional conceptions of learning, and discussing the implications for educators of independent patterns of learning will be of general interest to continuing educators.

Knowles, M. S. *Self-Directed Learning: A Guide for Learners and Teachers.* New York: Cambridge Book, 1975.

A short handbook implementing the andragogical principles outlined in Knowles's earlier books, this volume is one of the books most often used in continuing education. Knowles analyzes the teaching–learning skills needed for self-directed learning and offers a number of practical exercises for teachers and learners.

Marshall, L. A., and Rowland, F. *A Guide to Learning Independently.* Milton Keynes, England: Open University Press, 1983.

Written as a handbook for students (including adult students) entering formal courses of study, this work recognizes the importance of informal learning and advises learners to build its style into their formal learning activities.

Smith, R. M. *Learning How to Learn: Applied Theory for Adults.* New York: Cambridge Book, 1982.

This book is the result of its author's many years of research and practice in the area. Smith begins by analyzing critical characteristics and optimum conditions of adult learning, then reviews how adults can be helped to learn how to learn. He devotes chapters to self-directed learning, to learning collaboratively, to learning through educational institutions, and to alternative learning systems, and he concludes with a series of training exercises, including training for self-directed learning.

Smith, R. M. (Ed.). *Helping Adults Learn How to Learn.* New Directions for Continuing Education, no. 19. San Francisco: Jossey-Bass, 1983.

This sourcebook collection of case studies describes implementations of Smith's learning-how-to-learn concept.

Tough, A. M. *Expand Your Life: A Pocket Book for Personal Change.* New York: The College Board, 1980.

A marked departure from Tough's usual academic research, this small self-help pamphlet is divided into two parts. The first and longer part outlines some fields of knowledge, ways of deepening personal relationships, and possibilities for spiritual growth and makes some suggestions for increasing one's enjoyment of life. The second part encourages the reader to consider alternative personal futures.

Tough, A. M., Griffin, G., Barnard, B., and Brundage, D. *The Design of Self-Directed Learning.* Toronto: Department of Adult Education, Ontario Institute for Studies in Education, 1981.

A collection of papers reprinted from journals, this book is packed with practical examples of workshops, seminars, and curricula. The skills of self-directed learning are outlined, and applications of these skills in the postsecondary sector, at community colleges, and in medical schools are described.

Watson, D. L., and Sharp, R. G. *Self-Directed Behavior: Self-Modification for Personal Adjustment.* (2nd ed.) Monterey, Calif.: Brooks/Cole, 1977.

Written from an operant conditioning perspective, this book—for Skinnerians and others who enjoyed *Walden Two*—outlines a general theory of behavior, presents exercises for developing skills in self-analysis, and explores the link between self-directed change and professional help.

Stephen Brookfield is assistant professor of adult and continuing education and associate director of the Center for Adult Education at Teachers College, Columbia University, New York City.

Index